FOOTPRINTS THROUGH THE DESERT

BLAZING A TRAIL
OF PERSONAL TRANSFORMATION
THROUGH LIFE'S SHIFTING SANDS

BY
JOSH KAUFFMAN

THANK YOU

To my friends for helping me
And to my tormentors for teaching me:
You saved me one and all.

And a very special thank you to Dr. Mala,
without whom I would not be here today.

Table of Contents

Introduction

The story you are about to read is not important. It starts out with the sort of petty emotional drama that makes up most peoples' lives. Most likely the protagonist in this pitiful little tale will try your patience. After all, he is obsessed with his own little story and seems to devote most of his attention to building mountains out of molehills— repeating the same thoughts over and over again. Even a bit of perspective will reveal that his sad story was as easily escapable as in a James Bond supervillain's plot. Just as he put himself in that situation, he could just as easily have found the obvious way out. All in all the teller of our rather common and unremarkable story is a pitiful, obnoxious little fellow who happens to have been me.

If you find yourself getting wrapped up in the drama, you will likely remind yourself that on any bookshelf there are an infinite number of more important and truly sad stories about war and peace, life and death, disease and genocide, violence and poverty. You would be correct. Indeed, the words that follow and the story they contain are not the significant part, and the stakes in this case were not very high. It was one guy's sad little life for a few years when wars were fought and won, epidemics raged, and humanity's population increased by 400 million.

What matters here are neither the events nor the words, but the truths evoked. These truths changed my life and delivered me from an existence of intense suffering. My hope is that some can read this, recognize these truths, and change their lives through them. Even if one reader can change, so can all of humanity.

§

The unceasing dance of the universe's uncountable charged atoms creates a life force pulsing through everything. A veil, however, had always obscured its vitality from my vision. One day, the veil slipped, revealing to me for the first time both the veil's own existence and a world I never had really seen or experienced. I had learned empathy from someone who had none. I had learned how to live from those too consumed by their own fears and injuries to stop and live consciously, free from the pretentions and protective walls that held them fast. Without even realizing it, I had managed to slough off the weight of thirty years of grievances, injuries, and insecurities; to stand tall, and for the first time to feel life's radiant sun warming my face. All of the problems and complexities and narratives of my life had crested in an unstoppable tidal wave that nearly destroyed me—but then quickly receded—leaving in its wake an unassailable peace. Along the way came a thousand little lessons, like footprints in the sand leading through the desert to the Promised Land. These lessons I wish to share with you that they may show you, too, the way to a better life. They are not mine to teach but rather ever-repeating teachings expressing themselves through my story, as they do everywhere, all of the time. Thus, there are no new ideas here: just the old, timeless ideas revealing themselves in a new way through my own experience.

So, forgive me for my sad little story that comprises the first part of this book. Maybe you will see some of yourself or relate to it through someone you know, and maybe it can serve to bring to life the lessons in the second part. Or, maybe you will find it tiresome and completely unappealing. It is my tool such as it is: the instrument that revealed to me the truths in the second part, which are all that really matter. So, I give you the choice—you can try and relate to the tiring melodrama of the first section or skip immediately to the second section, whose truths stand on their own, although they may be, at times, lacking in context.

Part I

Chapter 1 - When all else failed

I arrived in Singapore, just about as far away on earth as I could possibly be from New York, where I was born and raised. Twenty-six years old, I had just graduated at the top of my class from one of the best graduate schools in international affairs in the United States. My 3.90 GPA had suffered a single B+, the lowest grade I ever received in my higher education. This had occurred during my last semester of school, when I already had a prized corporate job at a top international consulting firm waiting for me after graduation. I had also graduated with a 3.94 from one of the top undergraduate programs in international affairs in the country and previously worked in investment banking at one of the most competitive financial institutions in the industry. I had been a White House intern, had met numerous world leaders, had lived in half a dozen countries, and had traveled to dozens more. Given years of gainful employment during school, I had relatively little college debt and was about to receive a six-figure salary. I was healthy and fit. Select your own cliché: I was living the dream, the world was my oyster, I had it all.

My industrious parents had taught me the value of perseverance and education, so I did know hard work. And because failure was something alien to me—a mere mental concept—my imagination was forced to instantly commandeer convincing parries to that formulaic punch deployed by all job interviewers: "Give me an example of a failure you've faced in life and how you overcame it."

It was only there, at the starting point of what promised to be a charmed adult life, that I began to encounter almost nothing but failure and the suffering it brought. What followed was a five-year period of relentless bad news: sickness, trouble at work, heartache, melodrama, and a near total cessation of all of the hobbies, activities, and connections that seemed to give my life meaning and happiness.

When I first landed in Singapore in August 2008, I was already suffering from a terrible flu that would just not go away. Caught in a hell-raising rainstorm while waiting for some marquee tennis matches (eventually cancelled and tickets not honored) in the Beijing 2008 Olympics, I developed a cough that quickly degenerated into terrible congestion and a high fever. I had never really been sick before or to a hospital for anything other than a couple of stitches, and suddenly I was in the doctor's office every few days. Although the symptoms subsided somewhat, they made my transition into my new job and home more than difficult. The illness, however, never really went away, and I was forced to miss my first company retreat in Bali around a month after my arrival, due to what developed into severe pneumonia. At the time the doctor told me that the pneumonia was so advanced that I likely would have died in my sleep of asphyxiation had I not gone to the hospital that afternoon.

My recovery took several weeks, during which time I was absent from work and largely without visitors, as new to the city as I was. Though I felt much better, I was still constantly nagged by extreme congestion, even worse than the undiagnosed but very real respiratory problems that had slowed me down and prevented me from sleeping properly my whole life. So, with my gold-plated corporate health insurance plan, I finally decided to go to an ear, nose, and throat specialist to see what was ailing me. According to the doctor, if one's upper respiratory system were supposed to be a five-lane highway, mine was a dirt path. From my neck up, everything that could possibly be wrong was wrong. I had enlarged tonsils and adenoids and a deviated septum in my nose. Years of chronic sinusitis had led to a swelling of the flesh in my breathing passages and sinuses, causing terrible headaches. I had pockets of air and all kinds of abnormalities in the tissue surrounding my airways. The immediate causes of my suffering were the sinuses themselves, which were so swollen and infected that they did not have a cavity at all, but instead were distended outward into my nostrils. The congestion this caused had previously affected merely my sleep and breathing, but now the swelling was so acute that this severe infection was trapped in my sinuses, and it threatened to constantly re-infect me. This was all discovered after I got a urinary tract infection, an extremely uncommon affliction for a male.

The doctor wanted to give medication a chance, but my body did not respond to antibiotics, changes in my diet, a de-dustification of my house, or various and sundry medications. At that point, the only alternative was a complicated surgery. This was finally scheduled for February of 2009.

Mirroring my health during these first six months of the beginning of my new life, my career had taken a turn for the worse. I had been a star student like all of my new colleagues, but what set me apart from them was my previous work experience in an investment bank and elsewhere. Though a world-class education is invaluable in landing a top corporate job and developing critical thinking and communication skills, any veteran of the corporate world will tell you those first couple of years at a job—almost any job—teach you a professionalism that can be acquired only through experience. So, though brilliant, my colleagues were mostly fresh out of school and wet behind the ears. This gave me a leg up—or so I thought.

Unfortunately, at that time what mattered most in my workplace were relationships. If you ingratiated yourself with partners or managers, you would be staffed on a good project. If not, nobody knew who you were, and given the project-based nature of the work, you had little opportunity to prove yourself otherwise. The problem for me and a couple of my colleagues was that most of the new joiners had previously done internships with this office and hence were known to the partner-manager group. So they were staffed on project after project, while the several of us sat around week after week doing nothing, usually not even coming to the office. It was nice for a while to get paid not to work, but too soon this became quite a stressful situation: I became anxious that I was not learning anything or gaining any exposure to the business.

Then, to make things worse, my first task was a mini-project that did not go well. From the very beginning my manager on that project, herself in poor standing within the company, ranged from being dismissive to being outright hostile. Given the remarkably flat, accommodating, and friendly office culture, this was surprising. This particular manager made a significant error with respect to our nondisclosure agreement with a key global-perspective client, a move that could be a career-ender. She asked me to make a particular phone call that just smelled wrong to me, but I had not seen our agreement in writing and hence was not certain of the specifics. When I challenged her, she became angry and sarcastic. Due to the performance pressures I was now feeling, I made the call. Sure enough, when I reported it to the partner, it was a huge problem. This issue nearly cost us the client. When confronted, I clearly stated what happened and that I had been instructed to make the call despite my objections. For her part, the manager did not blame me outright but also did not take full responsibility. Hence I was put on probation. The partner, notorious in the office for his pettiness and arrogance among an otherwise down-to-earth and extremely approachable group, was also in charge of the broken staffing system. He made it clear that he would see to it that I would not get staffed again. He lasted a couple of more years at the company. The manager was never staffed on client work again and left a few months later.

This whole mess occurred from December of 2008 through January of 2009, alongside my nagging illness and preparation for surgery. I went traveling in Malaysia with some friends for Christmas and New Year, but the situation was waiting for me when I returned. My officially appointed mentor was concerned with my situation and proactively brought me onto his team, during which time I helped out on random tasks. Unfortunately, he also was not very well thought of in the company, and he too soon left. At that time, I was left with no supporters, and the project itself fell apart. In the depths of the financial crisis, I was again unstaffed.

At the same time, my social and romantic life those first six months in Singapore had been a string of unfortunate events. I had a few old friends there, whom I knew from the time I had lived in Hong Kong a few years earlier, so I was not totally alone, but I had some trouble relating to my younger colleagues. I also had a sort of boyfriend, a friend of a friend I had met and taken to a few years before during a visit to Singapore. We had corresponded during my time in graduate school, and by the time I returned to Singapore, we fell very easily into a relationship. The honeymoon, if there was one, was very short. I immediately saw a surprising side of him: a vicious, unpredictable temper, a global pessimism and negativity, and an obvious self-loathing. Our relationship lasted all of one month before I ended it. The few friends I had all stated their relief, given his association with social drama. Apparently, in his social circle he was notorious for being psychologically unstable. I wondered why I had not been warned earlier!

At this point, combined with all my other false starts, it had not been a propitious beginning to my time in Singapore. Sure, I was glad to have extricated myself from a bad romance before we became too involved, but at the same time breaking a relationship with someone I had known and with whom I had corresponded for years was not easy. I had always been something of a loner and misfit, and my hidden sexuality had made my childhood and adolescence a lonely and uncertain time. Also, I had always felt stuck in between my other siblings. My older brother, much taller and more athletic than I, had always been my mother's golden boy. As is often the case, my mother had taken her oldest son to be the new man in her life as her relationship with her husband grew more distant. My twin sister was the typically prized only girl, coddled by both parents. My younger brother had been the baby, a role even further strengthened by a terrible and rare illness he suffered as an infant. Not only was he my father's favorite, but his status as youngest attracted a particular sympathy from both parents, who had both been the babies in their families. As such, I was the consummate middle child, and even in my own family had always felt alone. So, I came to strongly value human connection, seeking and being content with having one or two intimate and meaningful relationships at a time rather than a large social circle of friends. Hence, breaking a relationship, however unhealthy or unsustainable, was always a difficult thing for me.

Nevertheless, I was reasonably confident socially, in better physical shape than I had ever been, and comfortable with my homosexuality. In this new country I felt free of the personal history I had accumulated, the series of roles I had played when trying to establish my adult personhood as an adolescent and college student. So, I went out and made a concerted effort to meet new people, even through the trauma of this latest broken relationship and my health and professional troubles. I soon met another guy. That went well for a week or two, but in November of 2008, when I went on a long business trip and Thanksgiving break in the United States, he promptly emailed me and told me he was no longer interested.

I was feeling overwhelmed when I returned to Singapore in late November. Both my professional and personal lives were going relentlessly downhill, and I was still facing a long and intractable illness. You can imagine the boost my ego got when out of the blue a supremely eligible bachelor contacted me via Facebook, wanting to meet me. A writer, Jonah was intelligent and intellectually curious as well as dashingly handsome. He noticed my profile because we shared several completely random friends, none of whom had anything to do with each other, and he was quite upfront in saying he found me attractive. To me—after a string of failures—this seemed a small personal victory. Finally I felt like something good had happened.

As odd as it may seem for a homosexual relationship, our court-ship was quite old fashioned. Jonah and I met for coffee. We had nice dinners and went to the theater together. He was smart and funny, and we had a lot to talk about. He could keep up with my diverse intellectual interests and was the first person I had met in a long time who was proactively seeking to spend time with me, rather than the other way around. He introduced me to his group of friends, which consisted of a lot of smooth talkers and well-connected young professionals and, given his career, a lot of the local glitterati, A-listers, and cultural elite. Sooner or later, on the fourth, fifth, or sixth date, our relationship became intimate. For me, it seemed effortless, like the beginnings of any relationship should be. We were connecting well and learning more about one another for a month or so. It was just simple, fun, and nice, a comforting respite when everything else was going wrong. I told Jonah that I was looking for a relationship and was interested in seeing where things led with him, and he said the same.

But, like everything else at the time, this warm and fuzzy period did not last for long.

On one of those first few dates, Jonah mentioned that he was recently out of a relationship. Then, the next date, it actually turned out the relationship had been quite a significant one, which had lasted some years. They had been living together. In fact, they were actually still technically living together while Jonah was moving his possessions out. The holiday season arrived, and I took my holiday trip in Malaysia with some girlfriends. When I returned, the drip-drip-drip regarding Jonah's boyfriend continued. By the time Chinese New Year rolled around, Jonah confessed that he was kinda-sorta-maybe still in a relationship with the guy, Nelson, and they were going to Bali together to see if they could work it out.

Obviously I was not pleased. This short relationship was the one thing that seemed to be going right in my life, especially because my troubles in the office had reached a dramatic turning point, when I was officially put on probation. For me, however, at least it would be a resolution: Jonah would either leave the guy once and for all after this trip, or they would patch things up and get back together. All I asked was that Jonah keep me in the loop. No drama.

Those were anxious days for me. The Chinese New Year holiday ended with no word from Jonah. I called. We were going to meet up. At the last minute, Jonah cancelled, saying Nelson had come to his office and made a big scene that he needed to clear up. Another attempted meeting ended similarly, with Jonah backing out right before I was to meet him. A week passed with no word.

Although I was trying desperately to hold on to the one thing that had seemed to be on track in my life, I was now facing the surgery, and I was scared. A friend called me. I went out and did the one thing that I could think of to take my mind off of things—I got completely drunk. In my stupor, as could be expected, I started to feel the emotions I already felt, but with a greater intensity, and I lost my inhibitions. By pure coincidence, I met a guy named Nelson, and despite my intoxication realized it was Jonah's Nelson, whom I had never met or previously even seen. It set me off. It was classic drunken drama as I texted Jonah a series of nasty messages, and for the first time in over a week, he was responsive. It seemed he had recommitted to his relationship, and the petty alcohol-fueled drama I had created gave him the perfect excuse not only to end it with me, but to blame everything on me as well. He had never been really interested in me, he admitted. He claimed that we were not even really "seeing" each other and that I was delusional to even think that we were. Amazingly, he claimed to have been honest about his relationship all along. Because he had already introduced me to his friends at multiple venues, it was not difficult to imagine that people assumed something was going on between us, as in fact it was. Yet, he accused me of spreading rumors purposefully to destroy his existing relationship, an odd charge considering that he had only recently told me he was still kinda-sorta-maybe still with the other guy. After a back-and-forth that lasted a couple of days, he was pretty upfront with me, saying point blank that all along he had just been looking for some fun while he was repairing his relationship and that he never had any feelings for me or intentions of cultivating anything deeper.

This was the last straw. My life was an utter mess. I was one mistake away from losing my job, I had been sick on-and-off for six months, facing the first major surgery in my life, and every relationship of any kind I had attempted to build had come to an unpleasant end. Someway, somehow, everything had quickly gone all wrong. For about a week, I ceased to function, which presented no immediate problem because I was not working. The stage was set for a major depressive episode, but when all else failed, a new hope appeared in my life.

Chapter 2 - Salvation, bliss

My surgery was a few days away, and I was in a terrible emotional state. However, though I had nothing to occupy my days, a true depression did not have enough time to fester. In mid-February of 2009, the last weekend before going under the knife, I once again did the only thing I could to take my mind off of all that had happened—I went out drinking. To try and distract me from everything, a friend invited me to a birthday party. It was a low-key affair at an al fresco wine bar, with maybe a dozen guests. And there he was—a classic, tall, dark, ruggedly handsome, and well-dressed guy. I can still picture him leaning against a pillar by the bar, his diamond-stud earring glinting in the lamplight, the smell the cologne on his collar, neither cloying nor too faint. Peter his name was. He had a wry smile as he listened to me. He was not taciturn, but sparing with his words, contributing just enough to show he was listening and keep me wanting more. I told him of my upcoming surgery, and he said he would visit me in my recovery. At that point, he looked to be the only one who would. This was another hungrily welcomed distraction.

I went in for surgery a few days later. Although I had been under general anesthesia during the procedure itself, and there was no pain in the immediate aftermath, the recovery was much longer and more painful than I had anticipated. I was bleeding through my nose for weeks and needed to go to the doctor daily and then every two or three days for a month. The healing was going much more slowly than even the doctor expected. I was physically exhausted, maybe from blood loss, and my recovery was interrupted by a couple of sinus infections, which were extremely painful because my internal wounds were still open. A close friend from overseas visited me for a few days, and one of my colleagues dropped by, but other than that I was alone—except for Peter.

Less than a week after my surgery, Peter came over and brought me dinner. He was back a few days after and then again after that. He accompanied me to the doctor, an unpleasant experience given that the main event at these follow-up visits was to suck the excess blood and congealed matter out of my sinuses. He was totally unfazed and even curious to see what was going on with my recovery. At some point we kissed. Besides the fact that any attention or human connection would have been a great comfort to me at this point, that this dreamy guy took such an obvious interest in me even in the grotesque state I was in was a godsend. When everything had fallen apart in six months, once again a guy offered to rescue me.

After a few weeks, despite the blood, I was functional. I returned to work. My official mentor was leaving the company, but I found that I would be staffed on a short but exciting project in South Africa, a country I had always wanted to visit. Off the most aggressive painkillers, I could go out and even drink. Very soon Peter became my constant companion, and very soon we became intimate. He introduced me to his friends. He introduced me to his oldest and dearest friends. We shared dinners, and he checked up regularly to see how I was doing. It all fit so naturally, like a hand in a glove. Salvation.

Six weeks or so after my surgery I went to South Africa, and Peter and I spoke regularly during those three or four weeks I was gone. The project had been a success, and I immediately got my next staffing in Singapore, a rarity considering that ninety percent of the projects involved weekly travel. I was back on track at work. The partners, whose only impression of me had been formed by the one unfortunate incident leading to my official probation, began to take notice of my performance. As had been my expectation, my professionalism and communication skills, developed from years of working in Washington, D.C. and in investment banking, began to pay dividends.

At the same time, my relationship with Peter progressed steadily and without impediment. He began sleeping over during the week, which was also convenient for him because he lived with his parents, as far away from the city center as you could possibly be without leaving the country. His office turned out to be right across the street from mine, so we saw each other frequently, though, given my extremely long hours in the office, we rarely commuted together. I found him to be such a reassuring and refreshing presence in my life. Not only was he fastidiously attentive and deeply interested in me, he was different than anyone I had ever known. Having attended top universities and working with extremely intelligent, driven, and opinionated people, I was accustomed to strong personalities with firmly held beliefs. Talking was usually debating, and social interactions were often about who came out ahead at the end of the point of contact. This was the nature of social interaction among the jetset business and elite academic crowds to which I had become accustomed.

Peter was different. Intelligent and intellectually curious, he had nevertheless attended university late, in his mid-to-late twenties. He had been a poor student and a problem child during his adolescence. However, having gotten himself back on track, Peter had a certain level of cultivation and professionalism that gave us enough in common to serve as a platform for building a relationship. Yet, rather than demonstrating his intelligence by scoring rhetorical points and engaging in intellectual jousting, Peter asked incisive questions. He did not have the depth of knowledge to formulate and reinforce hardened opinions about many political, social, and other issues. Instead, he listened well and offered his thoughts after consideration. At times, my certainty and confidence melted away when confronted with his fresh perspectives. The combination of open-minded nonpartisanship in his approach to what I considered to be serious topics, along with his obvious intelligence, stopped me in my tracks. It was the je ne sais quoi of my attraction to him. That, plus his good looks and great cooking, won the way to my heart. I loved him. It was the type of love that so many people have written of and to which I cannot add anything more eloquent. I fell asleep loving him and woke up still in love. My heart melted a little bit just at the sight of his smile, and my body warmed at his touch.

Our relationship progressed, and I was buoyed by rapidly improving performance and a higher status at work. The good fortune I had to actually be staffed on a Singapore project for the next six months gave me the opportunity to see him on a regular basis. Our relationship was drama free during this time, and we struck a nice balance between domesticity and an active social life on the town. When I moved apartments in September of 2009, he more or less moved in with me. Bliss.

Chapter 3 - The trap

My first oh-shit moment with Peter occurred sometime in the late summer of 2009, when he began sharing more with me regarding his past. It turned out that his adolescence and young adulthood had been more than problematic, venturing into the sordid and destructive. In fact, it was the stuff of an episode of Jerry Springer combined with a porno flick. Peter had never had a monogamous relationship before me, and then, at age thirty-one, he had been a regular at gay saunas and sex parties. During his relatively recent university days in Australia, he had been a frequent drug user and even dabbled in gay prostitution—not as a patron however. Because he had become active in the gay scene in his later teen years, Peter had slept with dozens or maybe even hundreds of men and boys and did not have an exclusive relationship with a single one of them.

As Peter revealed these and other facts, I formulated, with his encouragement, a story of his life. As with most gay people, his youth had been an awkward and uncertain time, which was not helped by his poor relationship with his quick-tempered father, who was away for months at a time working on a ship. Neither of his parents particularly encouraged him academically, and he had an undiagnosed learning disability, so he was a poor student. He was a teenager in conservative Singapore in the 1990s when the gay world existed on the margins of society at underground bars, bath houses, and discreet public places where gays cruised for sex. Scared and with no positive role models, like many gay youths in this type of environment, Peter fell under the influence of the wrong people. He met much older men who taught him "how to be gay," in other words, lacking any and all sexual restraint, shunning loving relationships, and taking on effeminate affectations.

Disturbingly, Peter met some of these people when he was brought into a perverse kind of church that encouraged this type of behavior. Though I cannot say I know well or fully understand the teachings, as Peter and some others explained them to me, the church taught that Jesus changed the world and hence the religious traditions that came before him, including all of the commandments in the Old Testament, which were therefore null and void. If you accepted Jesus, you were saved—this is a core tenet of many denominations of Christianity. However, what this church seemed to add was that as a follower of Jesus, all of your actions were therefore part of God's will. In the absence of any theological law, not only were any of your actions not sinful, but they were actually right because you were a believer. The religion automatically justified whatever the church members did—gambling, drinking, carousing, whatever—as long as they believed in Jesus.

As surprising as it may seem, there are a number of mostly Chinese churches that seem to teach this kind of belief system in Singapore, where the need for social affiliation is strong because the collapse of Confucian values and traditional Chinese social structures left a void in people's lives. What made matters worse was that Peter's church was an explicitly gay affair, and hence it seemed to serve as a hookup joint where older gay men had access to a pool of confused and outcast teenage boys looking for acceptance and a sense of belonging. Not only was Peter taken advantage of by these much older men, but the situation continued long after he stopped attending regularly. The pastor at the time I lived in Singapore was a gay man a few years older than Peter who was a regular on the gay social scene, usually with one or several much younger, troubled adolescents in tow. One of them was usually a boyfriend or fling—and often intoxicated. One can only imagine how in his younger years Peter and these other boys had been manipulated, taken advantage of, and influenced by the older members, and the impression it had left on their young minds.

This story was a tragedy to me, and it made perfect sense why Peter had gone to university later in life and had taken some time to get his life off the ground. Peter, however, had changed. He had held a professional job in public relations consulting for nearly two years when we met, and he claimed to be seeking a more stable social life, further evidenced by his relationship with me. Though he was initially a little surprised by my assumption that our relationship was exclusive, Peter went along with it, and overall encouraged my narrative of his life—he was a problem kid who had fought his way back and was building a responsible adulthood. This was a nice story we both created, and in fact telling it to myself made me admire and respect him even more. For myself and the cohort of people with whom I grew up, success came easily—our parents had money, and we grew up in an environment that fostered academic and professional achievement. We should have been smart and successful, and in fact we had no right *not* to be. Peter on the other hand had become so against all odds. He, who had overcome so much, lifted me up out of my sadness, whereas I was the one who had always had it so easy. He was my hero.

Unquestioningly accepting this story proved to be a major mistake that we will revisit in depth later. At this point, what I should have known, and indeed did already know but out of fear hid from my better judgment, was that even if the story were true, rehabilitation from a past such as Peter's is a process, not an event. Years of a hedonistic lifestyle and generally unrestrained behavior are extremely unlikely to become undone with the first relationship. The lifestyle Peter had lived for his whole adulthood until then naturally engenders some or all of the following: a lack of self-control, an inability to accept behavioral limits, a poor understanding of consequences, an inability to read or even have interest in emotional cues, and an underdeveloped sense of responsibility. These are things that normally take years (indeed the totality of one's youth, if not longer) to develop. My happy story said Peter had changed and that his job and relationship with me were proof of that change. So, I ignored my better judgment and continued on my merry way.

Meanwhile, though I failed to realize it at the time, the combination of my improving career and deepening relationship with Peter created a kind of trap, which I happily stepped into. After a time in my life in which suddenly for the first time everything was a failure, my relationship with Peter was a source of tremendous validation for me. At this time, as I began to work regularly, my job began to consume my life. Consulting is a highly glamorized career sought after by top MBA grads, but it is an extremely demanding life. In Asia, it involves 80+ hour work weeks and constant travel. So, my success in the office led to me sacrificing my social life almost entirely. I had no time for any of my hobbies—cooking, sailing, photography, writing— and instead spent nearly all of my free time with Peter and all of my efforts trying to make him happy, to ensure our relationship worked. I had little time for the few friends I had, who in turn also had busy lives and little patience for my crazy schedule. Though I did not realize it at the time, my entire identity and sense of self-worth became the combination of work plus my relationship. Descartes said, "I think, therefore I am." For me, it was "Peter is happy, and our relationship works, therefore I am."

To make matters worse, my health again declined. After I had recovered from my surgery in the Spring of 2009, my constant sinus infections returned. Prior to my bout of pneumonia, my chronic sinusitis had mostly been a quality-of-life issue, making breathing and sleeping difficult. Now that the surgery had opened up my air passages, at night the infected mucus from my sinuses dripped down into my lungs, causing frequently recurring respiratory infections. This became a serious health issue, as I suffered bronchitis or pneumonia every couple of months. As someone who typically went to the gym six days a week, I ate a lot. However, although I could not exercise with the lung infections, and my stamina was impaired in the weeks thereafter, my body still screamed for the calories. I would gain weight while sick and in recovery mode, lose the weight during a month of good health, and then gain it back when I got sick again. Constant traveling and eating in hotels, over my computer, resulted in a poor and erratic diet, and my weight would yo-yo as much as fifteen pounds during these two-to-three month cycles of health and sickness. The constant infection also permanently impaired my lung capacity, not dramatically, but enough for me to notice and limit my stamina while running.

Over the next few years I was afflicted with every manner of random health problem. An active person by nature, this severely limited my normal scope of activity. Hunching over the computer for so many hours a day, I developed deep muscle knots in my shoulders and back, causing imbalances in my muscle strength and poor posture. This led to severe seizure-like muscle spasms, necessitating trips to the emergency room for muscle relaxants and weeks at a time of recovery. I was eventually in constant pain that put me in physical therapy for years. Not normally a headache person, I developed a status migraine, essentially a killer headache that lasted for three months. Medication dulled the pain, but did the same to my senses, and hence I was living in a sort of continuous half-drunken state. I then developed some kind of eye infection that led to discoloration around my eyes, and somehow I caught a virus on my feet that caused painful growths. As someone who had never experienced so many health issues before, this was all frustrating for me and placed even more limitations of my social life and activities, to the extent that my insane work schedule even allowed for those.

The little that remained of my life outside of work and Peter did not provide any comfort. Though quite a long story, I had a classmate from Vietnam who was struck with cancer, and she had no other choice but to get medical treatment in Singapore. Having no family in Singapore, she stayed with a former professor who had relocated there. She had occasional visits from overseas friends and family members, but I was her only friend living in Singapore. I visited her as much as my work schedule, responsibilities to Peter, and my own health allowed—which was not very much. Her condition worsened over her year or so in Singapore, and I felt a tremendous weight as her only real friend who lived there. She eventually passed away, a young girl full of promise. It hit me very hard, and I was for a long time wracked with guilt. After all, what did all of those hours I spent in the office change? I could have made a dying girl's last months a little happier. At the same time, my friend's fiancé also passed away after a bout of cancer at a very young age, and she was forced to leave Singapore as a result. My family, though as far away as could possibly be, was also facing a challenge with my father's advancing Parkinson's disease. It was one bad thing after another after another...

So, my whole life as I had known it faded away, and I was pushed further and further into this trap of tying all of my personhood to my relationship with Peter and my incredibly demanding job. Over the next nearly three years, until the end of 2011, my only really happy experiences were during traveling. My work allowed me to combine exotic vacations with business. Likewise, under my influence Peter became quite the adventure traveler. Prior to our relationship, like many of his peers, Peter's idea of traveling was centered exclusively on eating, drinking, and shopping: no museums, outdoor or cultural activities, thank you very much. Given Peter's hedonistic lifestyle, sex meetups and drug-fueled orgies were another important ingredient of an ideal vacation before I came into his life. However, after a trip to Bali in which we largely avoided the formulaic beach-and-party tourist scene there, Peter's perspective changed. After that, we traveled together to Egypt, Ladakh, Kashmir, and some other exotic locations, and he took up photography. These escapes from reality kept me going in those years, and during long stretches of the mundane daily grind I was always looking toward the next adventure. I fell further and further into the trap.

Chapter 4 - Hanging on

By 2010, Peter was my everything. He was my savior. My relationship with him and career comprised the entirety of my life. I woke up in the morning to see his smile and made it through the day (or week, when I was traveling) so I could come home to put myself in his arms. I was a dry husk of a human being. My core, my passions, and dreams were hollowed out, especially as my interest in my job waned. Not surprisingly then, similar to my uncritical acceptance of the Peter-has-changed narrative that I myself had created, I ignored all of the warning signs that the relationship was not healthy. He was all I had, and I would hang on to him no matter what. I was nothing without him.

In addition to his family upbringing and homosexuality, Peter's past lifestyle was partially the result of some innate personality traits—his tendency to be capricious and temperamental. Peter's hedonistic lifestyle in turn reinforced these very traits. Not used to being responsible to other people or sticking with something through the good and the bad times, Peter would often randomly make all manner of pronouncements about what he was going to do. Bad day at work? He was quitting his job. He was moving too. To where? Taiwan! Taipei had a great gay drug-and-sex party scene (even though he did not engage in that anymore). No, China! Even though he had never been there, he was sure he would love it. By the time I met him, Peter was no longer capable of engaging in a logical or deliberate decision-making process based on a long-term goal or principle and executed with a rational connection between means and ends. He acted on impulse, which in turn made him even more impulsive, and in the end he simply could not function as a reliable partner.

Soon into our relationship, I made it clear to Peter that, although I was happy to stay in Singapore for some years with him, I did not plan to grow old and die there. In the first couple of years, Peter was in total agreement with me. He wanted to move to Australia or the US or Europe. When my company presented an opportunity to transfer to Australia, Peter was completely amenable, offering to open up a conversation with his boss to see if he could transfer to an affiliated company there. As soon as I initiated the formal process however, with no explanation Peter said he did not want to move there. Then, sometime in early 2011, more than two years into our relationship, Peter proclaimed he was never leaving Singapore. Though this was a deal breaker for me, I had learned not to take anything he said too seriously. However, any clear-thinking person, which I was not at the time, would have certainly seen that this was not someone who understood long-term commitment and mutual responsibility. There are no more *me* decisions in a relationship, only *we* ones. Peter did not understand this and, having lived the life he had, it is easy to see why.

We rarely fought, but our otherwise comfortable domestic life together was punctuated by a few instances when I thought it was all over, especially in 2011. On several occasions Peter suddenly pronounced that we should break up, each time with no obvious event precipitating the statement. When I inquired further or reacted emotionally, usually with tears, he would not have anything of substance to say and typically was not able to provide any coherent rationale for what he had said. By the next day, he seemed to have forgotten it all and was back to normal, and therefore, so were we.

Over time intimacy also became an issue. For me, sex was never a difficult thing requiring lots of conversation and thought, like it is for many people. We had a healthy sex life for the first year or so. However, it was not surprising to me that things slowed down after a while, given my constant illness or injury and work travel. But, it became less and less frequent. Then, in the last of our three years together, it stopped. Either randomly or whenever I brought up the issue, Peter would usually have an excuse ready that would often involve some aspect of my appearance that I should change—then we could have sex again. Dye your hair blond he said. Shave it. Wax your body. Get a tattoo. Bulk up. Lose weight. Though I did not realize it at the time, I had already lost all of my sense of self-worth independent of our relationship, and with it, my self-esteem. These frequent criticisms were partially a symptom of a larger global negativity very common among Singaporeans, a fact I had come to accept (a recent Gallup survey found Singaporeans to be the least positive people in the world). Peter's criticisms of my looks or anything else about me were rarely vicious or mean spirited, but there was simply no positivity. Having no sense of self anymore, rather than see that I deserved better or that this represented a real problem in our relationship, I just held on tighter.

So, I held on as the roller coaster careened steadily downward. I became increasingly desperate. I tried to talk to him, but given that he had never had a committed adult relationship and that his cultural milieu discouraged discussion of personal feelings, he was not much of a talker. I thought it would be okay, that I would make it work no matter what. Sometime in early 2011, I asked him to spend the rest of his life with me. He said, "That sounds nice."

Chapter 5 - The fall - part 1

I still remember the day when I realized I had to do something. It was mid-2011, after he had accepted my informal proposal. Peter was once again criticizing my looks, this time encouraging me to wax my stomach and chest. So, a few days later I did. He did not even notice. I asked him if anything was different about me. He had no idea. There was no ignoring it at that point—he was not even looking at me any longer. Not realizing how weak I was emotionally and how empty my life was without him, I steeled myself for the worst.

I resolved to confront him but found every reason to dither. It was the summer, and my lease was up in September, when I would certainly need to move out. Given the bargain rental rate I had gotten on the apartment at the lowest point in the financial crisis, there was no way the landlord would not sharply raise the rent. Why create drama ahead of that when we were still living together? It would be much easier to talk to him after we moved out. I had also expressed my intent to take advantage of a transfer program at my company that allowed employees to work in another office of our choice for six months, and I wanted to go to Paris. Peter was fine with my intention to do the temporary transfer, not surprising given that he was already checked out of the relationship. I was supposed to leave in August, even earlier than the September date of my move-out. So, I played pretend that everything was normal and tried to ignore my rising sense of dread.

August came, and my transfer was delayed to September and then to October and finally early November. I was going to confront Peter in September, but then he booked a trip to Vietnam for us with friends in early October, and I decided to wait until after that. I wanted to keep the peace and was holding out some hope that the trip could reignite things. Then I realized his birthday was right after the trip, so I delayed again so as not to ruin that. He moved into a shared apartment after I gave up my place at the end of September, and I was renting a room from my friends for my final month before the transfer.

Finally I could wait no longer. I had made up my mind months ago. I felt strong. I even told some friends that I intended to confront him and that I expected it would lead to a breakup. It was tough. But then, when the moment came, I clammed up. I wept more violently than at any time since I could remember. In between sobs, I simply told him that I could not live like this anymore, that I felt fat and ugly, that he was not interested in me. I needed him to recommit.

He did. Not with words, of course—his cultural background combined with his never having had a committed adult relationship in which he actually had to explain his feelings prevented him from finding anything to say. However, he began to stay with me when I moved in with my friends for that last month in Singapore, was extra attentive toward me, continued to spend all the time he could with me, and promptly bought tickets to visit me in Paris. What went down, now came up. The rollercoaster brought me back up high, and after so many months of dreading this moment, of steeling myself for it and then collapsing when the moment came, now all of that did not matter. He had recommitted.

I was ecstatic. I left for Paris at the very end of October, convinced now that the time apart would do us some good, but eagerly awaiting his visit. We talked a few times those first two weeks. Then, perhaps three weeks into my time there, he called me out of the blue and dumped me. He labored over his first inarticulate words, perhaps the first time in his life he had chosen proactively to express to another person his deeply held feelings, which are seared in my memory. "You're gone, and I realize I don't miss you, and I don't love you." The rollercoaster went crashing down again. Emotional whiplash.

I was devastated, so I did what I knew best—I traveled. I was immediately going back home to New York to spend Thanksgiving with my family and then had plans to travel with my mother to the famous Christmas markets of Eastern Europe for the year-end holidays. I kept myself constantly busy and somewhere harbored hope that when he visited in early January we would work things out. There were undoubtedly some tears, but mostly I was in a sort of shock. The realization that there was really nothing in my life that I was passionate about was slowly dawning on me.

I met Peter at the metro station in Paris after the winter holidays. He was wearing a hat I always loved on him but that he almost never wore when we were together. He really had nothing substantive to say to me. I kept waiting for him to say it was all a mistake, that he missed me terribly. Though I did not realize it at the time, I know now that however sincere my love for him was, the relationship had become my sole validation in life. So, even if we did not rekindle our relationship, I needed desperately to just hear something from him—that he appreciated the time we spent together, that he was sorry to see me go, that I made some impact on his life. I needed him to show me that I was important, that my life had made some difference, that I was a good person. At that point, I saw no other way of proving that to myself.

His words and actions said quite the opposite. His very first day he told me about his exploits in a gay sauna in Taipei. Doing the math about when that happened, I figured it could not have been more than two weeks after he dumped me—hardly the actions of someone with any degree of sentimentality about his ex. When I was at work, he met up for sex with people in Paris from gay websites. He told me about all of this, not even realizing how or why that would be painful for me to hear. He missed dinner. Everything he did and said screamed at me, "You are not important. You were never important." This was abundantly clear to me by the time he left. I was flying off to begin a long project in Helsinki, and similar to the way I had handled confronting him about our relationship, I waited until the very end to talk to him, hoping to keep the peace while he was in Paris and avoid unnecessary drama.

Peter arrived in the weeks after I returned from my travels in Eastern Europe, when I had no more adventures in the immediate future to anticipate, and the truth of my life situation, or at least of how I saw it at that time, hit me quickly. I had given my whole self to that relationship. I had made life decisions for Peter. Despite plenty of opportunities to leave, I had stayed in Singapore, a place I had grown to detest, for no other reason than to be with him. I had given up friendships and hobbies, neglected a dying friend. Peter was what had given my life meaning for those three years as everything else fell away. Peter's lack of reaction to the end of our relationship quickly put me into my place, but his callous behavior drove me over the edge. At our final parting on the way to Charles du Gaulle airport I told him how much he had hurt me over those years, how desperate I was to hold on to him, how I lived with the dread that I was not good enough for him. I felt fat. I felt ugly. I felt boring. I had given up everything for him. He had no reaction. That drove me further. What reaction could I expect from him, who had never had a committed relationship before, who had apparently slept with every man, woman, and child in Singapore? What did he know about feelings? What could I expect from him, who had never been responsible to anyone in his life? He did not say anything. That did it for me. I told him I never again wanted to see him as long as I lived, and it was true.

So there I was, aged thirty, having spent the last three years of my life giving my all to someone to whom I ultimately meant nothing. I was sick, out-of-shape, without any of my former hobbies or pursuits, nearly friendless. Throwing myself into work was really my only distraction, and indeed, given my demanding job, I did not have much of a choice anyway. However, I had long ceased to be interested in my job, so as much as it filled my time, it did not really occupy my mind and certainly did nothing for my soul. I flew to Helsinki week after week, where the particularly cold winter brought temperatures -10 degrees Celsius on a good day and perhaps two hours of daylight. I worked regularly until two in the morning, and the project was not going well. Returning to my hotel room alone each night, the silence was oppressive. The air, thick and heavy from the heating system meant to combat the subzero outdoor temperatures, was stifling. I very quickly fell into a state of despair.

In my flailing around for something—anything—to grasp on to, I did send Peter frantic and rambling emails trying to somehow make sense of what had happened. What he told me made matters even worse. His words surpassed my worst suspicions. With his typical flippancy he told me that he hadn't been "into white guys" for a long time by the time he met me but never thought to tell me that. So, not only was I heartbroken, but it was over someone who did not really care about me to begin with, based on the color of my skin. I had given up my whole life and passed up countless opportunities for joy and advancement—all for someone who knew the whole time we were together that he was not interested in me. In this case, both the intensity of my love for him and my suffering at the loss were meaningless. Meanwhile, he had no obvious emotion, not surprising because, according to his own admission, his feelings for me had lasted for only a brief period near the beginning of our relationship. It all must have been a terrible bore for him, and the end should have come as quite a relief. I was alone in my grief and humiliated.

The five months of my life from January to May of 2012 is a blur. Work, hotel, work, hotel, work, hotel. As usual, I traveled a little to distract myself: easy for me considering I was in Europe and working for an airline. However, my heart was not in it, and I remember almost nothing from that time. The main hallmark of this period was a general sense of listlessness and ambivalence toward my future. I found myself sobbing at random moments, triggered by the slightest reminder of my defunct life.

Chapter 6 - Redemption?

By April of 2012 I was in the midst of trying to prepare for the unknown to come: my return to Singapore to—who knew what. At the time, out of the blue, two rays of light struck me unexpectedly, both promising to deliverance—before throwing me back down. First, Oliver, an acquaintance in Singapore with whom I had lost contact, got in touch with me. With no one else to speak with, I confided in him what was going on in my life, and his listening and sharing provided me great comfort while sitting at my computer during those wee-hours work nights. At twenty-seven, he was an artist, lecturer, and small business owner—hard working and creative. Like me, he had lived all over the world.

And then followed even better news, which had the potential to right the great wrong of my life in Singapore: that I had given up a slew of professional, personal, and romantic opportunities to be with Peter, someone who knew he didn't care for me for most of that time. Several years before, I had met a man named Gary when a friend invited him to a party at my house. Our encounters were brief, but I was quite taken with him. Though quiet, he was strikingly good looking and quite the talk among gay circles in Singapore. Beyond his looks, he was successful—in finance, and as a writer and part-time model. He was perhaps the It Boy of those few years in Singapore gaydom. Gary and I met several times by chance at social events, and we had always connected very well, but both of us were also in committed relationships. I was always struck by the intense eye contact he made when we spoke, as if he was listening intently and could understand me beyond my words. Like many people to whom I gravitate and vice-versa, he had lived an atypical life. He was

Taiwanese but had been raised in South America and educated in the US and UK. We found each other in crowded rooms, surrounded by all the vapidity and drama of gay social circles and had wonderful conversations about anything: politics, family, philosophy, religion, whatever. We went out to lunch and dinner a few times, and these occasions made the increasingly dull and droning days of my time in Singapore come to life. However, that was it. I went to France and did not hear from him.

That changed in April or May of 2012, when Gary suddenly contacted me. I was pleasantly surprised but confused. Why the sudden contact? Gary told me: Peter had been telling the news to people that he and I had broken up. Rather than fessing up to what really happened, however, he either lied outright or led people to believe that I had simply moved away and left him: the same familiar story as with many expat-local relationships—gay and straight. This was a convenient lie for Peter and cast him as the victim. Quite simply, Gary did not believe this and wanted to see if it were true, because he didn't think I was "that kind of person." However, the next bit of information proved more telling and even more interesting: Gary had also just broken up with his boyfriend. Was this my chance for redemption?

Apparently so. Very soon Gary and I were exchanging five emails a day, pouring our hearts out about our relationships, sharing what we were going through, and revisiting many of the same sorts of topics we had found of interest in our previous interactions. He began to get both suggestive and overtly sexual with me. This was all the vindication I needed: perhaps Singapore's most eligible gay bachelor and someone with whom I just happened to connect very well was aggressively pursuing me. It seems all wrong in hindsight: two people both in the midst of what should have been painful transitions moving towards some kind of romance. However, in the grip of my despair, isolation, and loneliness, it was all I needed.

I returned back to Singapore the weekend before I was officially moving back in order to do some house hunting. After all, one of the luxuries of working for an airline was free business class tickets anywhere I wanted to fly. I had arranged to meet Oliver, who missed the meeting without explanation. However, I did spend a wonderful evening with Gary, engrossed in conversation mainly about where our lives had taken us and what we were both hoping to do with ourselves at this time of transition—mainly to settle down and start a family. Though I was extremely irked by Oliver's unexplained disappearance, my time with Gary felt natural and effortless. It gave me something to look forward to in a situation that otherwise felt like a terrifying leap into the unknown, without even the comfort of the empty shell of a life I had been living. Without Peter, I was coming back to the city I knew well but did not like. I was without any close friends or hobbies and working a job in which apathy had now turned into loathing. For the very first time in my life I was completely without direction or goals, tossed about by whatever chance presented. A possible future with Gary was now the pillar to which I helplessly clung.

At this time, another bit of instability was injected into my life when I was told that I would be staffed on a project in Bangkok for a number of months, meaning there was no sense in getting a house in Singapore at all, and I would not have an opportunity to reestablish my life there. So, my house-hunting weekend trip to Singapore became an opportunity to reconnect with the few people with whom I was still in touch and just observe how being there made me feel. Of course, my move to Bangkok for a few months also meant no immediate future with Gary, but at this point I really could not contemplate more uncertainty, and after all, it would be only a few months. He was a hot commodity, but given how intimate our friendship had become since reacquainted, I thought I could make it work. I could redeem what little remained of my life.

Chapter 7 - A desperate paradise

Very soon, upon my final return to Singapore, I was told the Bangkok project was off and I would be working in Singapore for the immediate future. This amounted to what would be for most people a big change. My life had become such that is did not faze me at all but presented me with an opportunity to try things out with Gary and figure out if I should extricate myself from Singapore. For me, the place was poisonous. I saw Peter everywhere he was and was not— in the little food stall we had often gone to on Sunday mornings, the riverside where we first met, the pretentious bric-a-brac store where we always liked to browse but never buy anything. It certainly did not help that within two weeks of my return I did see Peter at my very first social night out (with Gary) and my very first trip to the shopping mall. Seeing him punctuated with a big exclamation point the general sense of emotional heaviness the place held for me. I clung more tightly to Gary, who was happy to play the part of protector. He told me he liked taking care of people. I needed to be cared for by someone. He said that it was his personal goal to see me through the depression into which I had fallen. It worked.

Gary and I increasingly began to spend all of our free time together, though that did not amount to too much for me, given that I was again put on a series of extremely demanding projects, which at times kept me in the office for as much as a hundred hours a week. However, the time we did spend together was something like magic. Given the number of years we had engaged in brief and sporadic but intense interactions and our month-long very personal online correspondence, he felt like an old friend. He accompanied me in house hunting, and we found a beautiful apartment that was a newly reconverted tenement in what is one of Singapore's only neighborhoods with real charm: its gentrified slum-chic answer to New York's Meatpacking District. The apartment even had a large indoor-outdoor kitchen, perfect for Gary's picture-perfect cat. The five-minute walk from Gary's house was also a significant bonus. Gary spent a whole day with me helping me move and unpack my belongings from storage. Things were suddenly looking very, very good as I moved into my new home.

In some painful ways, my old life did inevitably begin to encroach on the new one I was trying to establish. First, in unpacking my things, I discovered Peter had taken a number of items I wanted. Beyond the simple inconvenience and expense of having my things taken, I was determined on principle not to let him keep them. After all, he had spent nearly three years living under my roof in a relationship in which I paid for most things, and most of that time he knew he had no interest in me romantically and would have no future with me. There was no way I was going to let him continue to benefit from me. Of course, he made it as difficult as possible for me to get my things back, necessitating multiple back-and-forth visits with people he appointed as go-betweens. The pettiness reached such a level that he had someone return my television without the controllers or necessary wiring, both of which he later returned on separate occasions. This was all very emotionally draining for me, but I had Gary for support. Next, Oliver showed up again in some attempt either to get attention or to disrupt my life. I met him for coffee, and he gave me a nonexplanation for standing me up. It all related to his current relationship (which he had never previously mentioned) that involved a lot of drama and turmoil, precisely what I was hoping to avoid in this new phase of my new life. I accepted this as an apology but did not wish to pursue any kind of further relationship with him.

On the home front, however, things could not have been better. Gary and I began spending nights at each other's houses. Inevitably, the relationship turned sexual. At first this was difficult for me. I had not had a sexual relationship since I lost Peter, whose unrelenting criticisms of my appearance had left me feeling embarrassed about my body. I had lost a lot of weight during my time in Europe, given how depressed I was, and I spent many days without even eating anything other than lunch with my colleagues. It was not a good weight loss though—along with the fact I also lost all of my muscle tone, which made me even more insecure. Gary, however, was wonderful during this time. As fit and toned as he was, he obviously found me attractive and said so. Though things seemed to be moving very fast, it did not feel odd. We had known each other for years, so there was a solid foundation for our relationship, which seemed to naturally flow from this.

Quickly Gary began to integrate me into his life, and I was happy to oblige. He introduced me to his two best friends, a lesbian couple and colleagues of his. The big move came when he invited me to Taiwan to meet his family at the end of July. Beyond the fact that this is a typical cliché big moment, this took on particular importance in the context of Gary's life. Without delving too deeply into the details, Gary's life had been an extremely tortured one. When he was only five or six years old, due to problems in his extended family, his mother and father were forced to flee Taiwan for South America, suddenly, in the middle of the night, with Gary and his infant sister. They had just about US$1,000 in their pockets to support themselves. He was subject to extreme poverty, long periods away from his parents, violence, physical danger, frequent relocations, and constant inconstancy and insecurity. He had been raped as an adolescent and, in a bizarre episode, quasi kidnapped and psychologically tortured for months five years prior to our meeting.[1]

Through all of this tumult, Gary's parents and sister had been his only source of consistent, reliable love and comfort. All of that shared hardship had fostered deep familial bonds, and the four of them were like best friends. However, the family was very Taiwanese (a peculiar mix of traditional Chinese culture and extreme Taiwanese nationalism, familiar to people who know that country well). I felt at home with Chinese culture and the Taiwanese situation and could speak intermediate Mandarin, but Gary warned me about inadvertently saying or doing anything to upset their sensibilities. So, the stakes and risks in terms of our relationship were high.

The days I spent with them were beautiful. Gary's sister and parents were among the warmest people I have ever met, and the love they shared, forged by all those years of difficulty, was palpable. Being in their presence as they showed me all around their hometown was like stepping into a warm summer day from a cold winter's night. There was just a caring, loving presence that permeated the air. We all seemed to connect wonderfully, and Gary was delighted. In addition, talk of a future family came very quickly. I had known for years that Gary was intent on starting a family, and given that he was well into his thirties, he was feeling an increasing sense of urgency—he set his deadline at thirty-five. I too wanted children, and Gary even discussed the possibility of his sister serving as a surrogate mother.

Over the course of that summer of 2012, time moved languorously: fuzzy, warm, and idyllic. I slept at Gary's place, and he slept at my place. We took his cat for walks, and he cooked me elaborate meals. We took a few short trips and watched bad movies together. We double-dated with his lesbian friends, who fast became my apparent friends, and I took them all sailing. We woke up late on the weekends, something normally extremely rare for me, and had long and lazy brunches. I was busier than ever at work, but Gary was my constant companion.

The sweetness of it all did not conceal but rather made the fact that Singapore was not the place for me even more obvious. After all, to feel as uneasy about the place as I did in the midst of such joy made the point that much clearer. I worried about this, because Gary was in the middle of getting his permanent residency. However, even this was not a problem. Gary and I discussed the issue and decided we could move to Hong Kong. I had lived there six years prior and loved the city, and it would be easy to transfer there with my company. For Gary, it was even closer to his family than Singapore, and he also liked Hong Kong during our trip there together, when I showed him some of the less-visited places I knew beyond the touristy stuff. He also was ready to change jobs, and I helped him prepare for interviews during a lot of the time we spent together. So, this was it—I was going to be in the city I loved with the man I loved. We had a future planned out. He was gorgeous and successful, and my high-powered and prestigious job would spoil me for choice when I decided to move on to something I enjoyed more. It was everything I could have hoped for. It was paradise.

A paradise it might have been, but it became an increasingly desperate one. You see, Gary's loving, attentive treatment of me was juxtaposed with disturbing and odd statements that he began to make with increasing frequency. While puzzled at first, I began to see these perhaps as little windows into the kind of worldview that Gary's so troubled and turbulent past must have engendered in him. For example, when talking about his former boyfriend in Taiwan, with whom he had been living for several years, he characterized his decision to leave the country while in the midst of their relationship in the following way: "I just left and really didn't care what he thought. That's how I live. I just move on. You really can't get too attached to people." Shocked to hear this, I asked if by saying he *didn't care* that he was using shorthand for *my boyfriend didn't want me to go, but I felt I needed to leave anyway*, not necessarily a callous or selfish statement. Probably realizing my dismay, Gary made an ambiguous and dissembling nonclarification. When I asked him directly why I should not be worried that he would do the same to me one day, he assured me that I was different.

However, I did bring up his two lesbian friends when discussing the difficulties of leaving Singapore. I was sensitive to the fact that he had led such a tumultuous life and probably highly valued friendship and stability, so I wanted to make sure he had thought it through carefully before agreeing to go with me. "Oh yeah, they're friends, but you always make new friends. That's what I do. I leave where I am every five years or so and just forget about the people there. You can't get emotional about it." When I asked again why he wouldn't forget about me, his answer was "because you're family now, and that's the most important thing. Family is all you can rely on in this world—it's the only thing that's permanent." And besides, he said they might be what he described as his "best friends," but they were also materialistic, not that smart and a variety of other deficiencies he found in them.

Now that I thought about it, he really didn't seem to have any close friends. I was acquainted with a guy in Bangkok in whom Gary had confided but rarely saw and only occasionally contacted. There were some other people who had come into and out of Gary's life during his six years in Singapore, but he did not have regular contact with them, and he also had harsh criticisms of them: he used words like *mean* or *stupid* or *losers* or the phrase *they had ulterior motives*. Some liked him in a romantic way and persisted in their pursuit of him, as some people in that situation do, annoyingly. He occasionally met some of these acquaintances from Singapore or those from overseas who came to Singapore, but these were just short visits, maybe a meal or a few drinks—and that was it. There did not seem to be any substantive conversation, and as soon as they were gone, Gary usually had as much criticism for them as he had nice things to say.

One such acquaintance was a lady friend of one of those annoying guys. She was a sweet lady in her early forties who it seemed had spent some time with Gary during his friendship with the annoying guy (who I later found out had also gone to Taiwan to meet Gary's parents). The lady had a never-ending battle with leukemia and had been regularly in and out of the hospital for years. Sometime in the summer of 2012 she was back in, and it appeared the end was near. Having been acquainted with her through several friends, I visited her one evening. The hospital was right down the road from my house and right across the street from Gary's. When he did not express any interest in going, I asked Gary if he would come. "No, I haven't seen her in a while," he said airily. "Besides, she's been sick a long time. It's not like this is anything new." It seemed quite an insensitive thing to say, but I supposed they were not as close as I had thought. Then again, none of the quick drop-ins Gary sometimes described as *friends* seemed to be either.

I really didn't know what to think. I supposed his understandable reverence for family and lack of confidence in other sorts of relationships probably made this a defense mechanism for him. Maybe he beat to the punch the sadness caused by broken and impermanent relationships by justifying the separation in advance or just not ever getting too close.

The past seemed overwhelming for Gary in every way. Once our daily routines became entangled, I noticed how much effort he put into grooming, and it seemed like the brightest moments in his life were when someone noticed or commented on his appearance. It made his day. When talking about the family he wanted, he kept describing the perfect-looking gay family: two toned, tanned fathers and immaculately dressed and coiffed athletic children. What seemed to go hand-in-hand with this was his own attitude toward compliment-ing others, which was the same as Peter's. That is to say he didn't do it. When I showed him my photographs or asked him to read something I wrote or how I looked, he remained silent—and getting him to say something complimentary was like pulling teeth. He seemed to think the kind words would diminish him in some way, that he was giving away some measure of his own self-worth in doing so. I soon discovered the probable cause of this in Gary's past as well. In looking through some old photographs of a skinny, awkwardly dressed collegiate Gary, he remarked something to the effect of "I used to be such a dork. I'm never going to look like that again." Another went something like this: "I remember being so skinny, and people picking on me for it. This is what I tell myself every day at the gym when I lift." More absolutely, one several occasions he simply declared, "I am vain. For me, looks are everything."

Beyond these statements, which centered around specific situa-tions but perhaps revealed something a little deeper in Gary's psyche, he also in the course of those months made a series of alarming pronouncements about his approach to life and his values. We were once discussing sexual mores, and it appeared Gary had something of an unrestrained sexual history, though not as lubricious as Peter's. However, we broached the subject of prostitution in the context of his having used a prostitute before in Thailand. I expressed my view that prostitution was wrong under any circumstance. Nevertheless, I thought reasonable people could disagree in the context of certain developed societies with regulated, sanitized sex industries, such as the Netherlands. In places like Thailand however, prostitution would in my view always be wrong because the prostitutes are often drugged, trafficked, forced into sexual slavery, and the like. By patronizing the sex industry while knowing this dark context, one would have to assume some of the responsibility for it.

Gary made a series of confused remarks about what was "right" and "wrong," "good" and "bad," and so on, so I asked him plainly what those words meant to him. He said good and bad, right and wrong were determined by the law. If it was illegal, then it was wrong—if not, no problem. This raised the obvious question—prostitution is actually illegal in Thailand, whereas it is legal in Singapore, with a number of different legal statuses in different countries around the world. Does simply crossing borders change morality? Does the government really determine right and wrong? To the first question, Gary replied that there actually and fundamentally is no right and wrong. "I am amoral," he said. To the second is answer was a yes. Might makes right. If you have power and therefore the freedom, you can and should do as you please. Anyway, he explained that it wasn't really a question of law but more of social acceptance. If people accepted prostitution in one society, he had no qualms about engaging in it. His motivation for wanting to sleep with the prostitute was chilling: "I wanted to see what it felt like to own someone and make them serve me."

Oddly enough, on one occasion when walking through Singapore's own sanitized, and legalized, red light district, Gary remarked how sad it was to see all the prostitutes standing there. I was puzzled because Gary had advocated and defended prostitution previously. When I reminded him that he had used a prostitute in a country where human trafficking was the norm, whereas prostitutes in Singapore had all willingly gone through a legal process, he didn't have a coherent response. The obvious difference between the two situations was that he could feel guilt about supporting prostitution in Thailand and hence defended it, while he bore no responsibility for the situation of prostitutes in Singapore.

The most notable of Gary's moral and philosophical pronouncements was without a doubt the most disturbing thing anyone has ever said to me personally. At the time, it gave me goosebumps. Now it makes my skin crawl to repeat it mentally. Beyond the first few sentences, I cannot remember the exact words he used, and some of it was interrupted by my questioning, but it went something like this: "Josh, the difference between you and me is that you are a good person. You think about how what you do impacts other people. I don't. With all that I've been through, I've learned what a hard and terrible place this world is. So, I do whatever I want to get what I want, and if I hurt someone else, that's really their own fault because they allowed it to happen to themselves. I've learned to be strong, and that's what I'm teaching them. You have to be strong in this world to achieve things, and you have to just not care who gets hurt along the way. They'll get over it, or they won't—it really doesn't matter to me." In hindsight, it is clear why this statement, as I have observed, often elicits a physical reaction of revulsion from the listener: it is a simple verbal expression of evil.

Shocked, I tried to think of how I could spin such a cold analysis in such a way that would make this abrupt expression of Gary's worldview more palatable. Remembering Gary's own experience of being raped as an adolescent, I brought out the familiar old rape trope: Does a woman who dresses provocatively in a seedy place late at night and walks home alone *deserve* to be raped? However ill advised her actions might have been, did she earn her victimization? Once again, Gary dissembled and obfuscated, probably realizing he had shown just a little too much leg.

However, I should have remembered Gary's own response to my shocked reaction when he first told me of his own rape. He had been only fifteen or sixteen. A much older, wealthy man he met online during the early days of the internet had flown thousands of miles to meet him. Gary, in his naïveté, had visions of some kind of white knight romance. The man actually held him down and forcibly penetrated him, kept him in a hotel room, and repeated the process some half a dozen times in a day or so. When I asked how that might have affected him, he said something to the effect of, "Not much. I mean, I fought the first time, but after that I kind of accepted it and maybe liked it too. I guess I sort of wanted it really, so..." Rape was his first sexual experience, and he could not even call it what it was. I realized this was a very hard, grim person indeed.

I was scared: scared of being alone again, of my life turning upside down again. It indeed did slowly begin to dawn on me that I was dating something like a sociopath, but he was *my* sociopath. I was confused. He had treated me with such sensitivity and care until then, at the same time as he was revealing his demented worldview. I didn't know what to think in the face of such cognitive dissonance. If I could just lock him in by getting him to make the move to Hong Kong, I reasoned, I was set. Remember, for Gary, family was everything, so if we could start one, he would never leave me. My suffering through my time and soul-draining work, my traumatic relationship with Peter, all my illnesses and physical pain, and my abandonment of all of my own pastimes and causes would have meant something. So, I would move toward making the family as soon as possible, and my happily ever after was set. This is what I desperately told myself as the specter of Gary's psychological and emotional derangement became increasingly clear. I could and would make this work. I had to.

The stage was set, and I was the star in my own dystopian story, in which our white-picket-fence future was the light gauze just covering the surface of a profound sickness—that of Gary's fundamentally twisted view of the world and my acceptance of it in my desperation to be loved. As is always the case in such narratives, the collapse of this unsustainable dissonance would provide the main drama of the story.

Chapter 8 - The fall - part 2

Our relationship proceeded on its fast clip toward relocation, marriage, and family. Meanwhile the rising sense of alarm I felt about Gary's emotional makeup was sounding a distant rumbling of thunder. All was moving according to plan, other than a few bumps in the road. The virus on my foot was not responding to the normal treatments, which were becoming increasingly painful and made walking difficult for twenty-four hours and uncomfortable thereafter. The doctor recommended quite an ugly surgery, which would involve simply removing the areas of infected flesh. This took on a greater urgency as the virus seemed to grow more resilient and spread more rapidly with each treatment. This would make walking difficult for weeks and take months to heal fully. On top of that, I began to travel weekly to heavily polluted Jakarta for work, and this was not benefitting my respiratory health. I got yet another sinus infection, which again turned into a chest infection, leaving me wheezing and weakened. It perturbed me that on these occasions Gary did not express sympathy—in fact, he demonstrated mild annoyance—and often proved unreliable in showing up and meeting me around my scheduled travel and medical appointments, when we had agreed to do so. This I chalked up to his having a larger perspective gained from all he had gone through—he knew not to sweat the small stuff and would stick by me when it was *really* important.

One Sunday night in October I kissed Gary goodbye. He had cooked a great dinner, and I needed to prepare for my early morning flight to Jakarta. He was to visit me in Jakarta that coming weekend rather than me returning to Singapore, and we were in the midst of booking tickets during Christmas and New Year for a safari in Tanzania. We booked the tickets on Monday or Tuesday, but then he abruptly cancelled his trip to Jakarta due to a scheduling conflict with an office party to which he previously had committed but forgot when booking Jakarta. Although this was not an absolute surprise, I had asked him to give me more warning than that if he was going to cancel, and I had difficulty getting a flight back to Singapore for the weekend on such short notice. I wrote him an email calmly saying that I was disappointed because I thought that was not very considerate of him, and he simply replied that we would talk it over when I got back.

I knew something was wrong when I arrived in Singapore and received his cryptic message when I offered to pick up dinner for him. He said that I wouldn't want to share dinner with him after our talk. The ten minutes it took him to get from his place to mine stretched on interminably. I was expecting a temper tantrum from him, which I had seen just once before. The setting sun was casting its dying rays into my kitchen, and I was sitting down on the sofa. He walked in the door, sat down, looked straight at me, and said words nearly identical to those I had heard through the phone on another continent nearly a year before: "You're gone each week, and I realize I don't miss you when you go. I don't love you. It's over." That was it. There was no hint of emotion or concern in his voice, no explanation, and there certainly had been no warning. He made to leave.

There was no screaming, crying, begging, or drama. The words just paralyzed me into a state of genuine shock. This was to the beginning of yet another long, blurry stretch in my life that would last some six months or so in which I can remember only little disjointed fragments of clarity, like shards of a broken mirror. From what I can remember, I asked him some questions: Why? Because I don't love you. When? I dunno. Can we make it work? No. What are you going to do now? Take a little time off and think things over, with two recent breakups under my belt. With that, he stood up to leave. I rushed over and put my arms around him. He gave me a stiff hug and said goodbye.

I really did not know what to do or think. The shock was still upon me. The one thing I do remember is leafing through the Tanzania travel guide I had just bought for our upcoming trip, which was sitting on the armrest of the sofa in preparation for a weekend of planning. Over what must have been an hour or so, an increasing frantic energy rose up inside of me, and I started to shake. I called literally everyone I knew in Singapore who I could speak to at a time like this. Not that there were a lot of them (I could count the people on this list with just the fingers of one hand), but as had been my luck the last five years, every one of them was out of Singapore at the time. I felt as if I would explode pent up inside the house, so I just stepped outside and started walking.

Maybe two hours later I found myself returning home from the city center, and it just so happened that the only road that directly linked my neighborhood to the center passed by Gary's house. I called him up. By this time, I had burned off some of my nervous energy, but I felt numb. He invited me upstairs and I was once again shocked by his reaction. He seemed elated. He made light little comments such as his cat missing me already, but he expressed not a shred of a sense of loss, regret, sadness, or anything. Once again, I cannot remember much, but the only slightly thoughtful or profound thing he had to say was that he needed a little time off to think about why he so quickly tired of me when he had made such deep commitments—to move countries for me, talk about starting a family, introducing me to his family, and so on. Other than that, he exhibited absolutely no emotion other than joy. Here was another person I loved, so happy to be rid of me. Later that night he even sent me a web link to some stupid song about killing your ex. I simply did not understand. He went from planning his future with me, booking a trip to Africa with me, to complete indifference dominated by a sense of happiness at getting me out of his life. I was confused and felt worthless and devastated.

The next day was much the same—numbness. I sat through an extensive two-hour health screening, shuttled from the blood test, to the electrocardiogram, to the examination, shifting one foot after the other behind the nurse like a robot. Saturday morning is when the collapse began. I awoke that morning to find at the top of my Facebook page pictures of Gary's social event that had conflicted with our Jakarta trip. So much for a time-out to ponder. He was shirtless, intoxicated, and obviously having a hormone-infused good time. I texted him. I didn't understand. Was he not even a little sorry to see me go? He responded quickly and angrily. In his mind I was a self-pitying clinger-on who loved dwelling on sadness. He did not let such things slow him down. No, he didn't miss me or regret anything. In fact, he had wanted me out a long time ago, and I was in denial by not seeing the signs, which were clear. I was once again at a total loss. Our romantic relationship had lasted at most five months—how could anything be a long time ago? What signs had I missed? Was it not two days before he dumped me that we booked a vacation together? How could anyone switch direction and experience this kind of loss so quickly without any discernible negative emotional reaction? In five months, we went from old friends to lovers talking of children and marriage, moving overseas with each other, and meeting his family. Then, in two days, he tired of my face. The next day, he dumped me with all the sensitivity of a butcher carving up a carcass. The day after that he partied, and the day after that had nothing but contempt for me. What kind of human being would react this way, and how could Gary find it strange that I was deeply affected? He knew the depth of what had just transpired between us but also my recent history with Peter and in Singapore generally. He was keenly aware of all of that, because we had discussed it at length and depth. We had been through a lot of it together.

It was when I flew off to Jakarta Monday that the panic struck me. I was alone again now. Totally alone. No friends I could rely on. No hobbies. A job I hated in a city I loathed. My body in revolt. Who was I? Where was I going? I must have cried fifty times in those few days. I left my tiny little windowless office at the client site at least five times a day to cry in the bathroom. Still no one was available for a talk with me. Facebook lit up with more pictures of Gary's festivities— funny antics in the office with his colleagues, a few mid-week nights out. How happy he must have been to get me out of his life. I composed my thoughts and wrote him a letter just explaining how I felt, which I intended to read to him in person. This was all too sudden for me, the emotional rollercoaster had taken one too many turns, and I fell off. I needed to hear from him the words that I never heard from Peter, that I meant something to him. That it wasn't my fault. That his life was somehow better because of me. That I was a person worthy of love and respect.

He did agree to meet me when I came home that week, and he came to my house with a face made of stone. I asked him to please sit down, and he took the same spot on the chair where he had broken the news to me the week before. Now that I was no longer in shock and at least had collected my thoughts into something coherent, I began to tell him how I felt—how sorry I was to see him go, how I was mourning the loss of yet another broken relationship and stillborn dreams of our future and confused at what had happened and how quickly it all went. Midway into my little monologue, he shouted at me. "I'm out of this! I don't care about you anymore! I said all I had to say!" Finally I felt something other than sadness, and I yelled back at him "Well I'm not out of it! I still love you and I need to hear something from you. I need to hear that..." and I proceeded with the list of things neither he nor Peter ever said to me. However, midway through I simply collapsed onto the couch in a hysterical and incoherent sobbing mess. Once I was able to quiet myself, he did say to me that he had once loved me and that "it was beautiful while it lasted." He then said: "You'll be alright." I assured him that I would be, but midsentence I once again broke down and started to fall to the floor.

For just a split second, his mask slipped. He ran to me to physically prevent me from falling. His lip trembled, and he said "No you won't be [alright]." He then put his arms around me, half to support my weight and half to embrace. Once I had stabilized, I stumbled over to the corner, where I had packed a bag of the belongings he had left at my house. I handed him the bag, and at once he recovered his martial bearing. He seemed embarrassed and frightened of his own split-second emotional reaction. He left abruptly. I then fell to the floor, where I cried myself to sleep.

The next few weeks were a rapid descent into hell. I was again on medication for my chest infection, and my foot surgery was looming. My shoulder was hurting a lot again, and I was in physical therapy several times a week. At some point I made a previously scheduled trip to Hong Kong that was supposed to be for house hunting for Gary and I. I thought a return to that city I loved and soon-to-be home might lift my spirits. Instead, I wandered the streets like a madman and left miserable after three days, realizing that the change of scenery would not be my salvation. Slowly my few friends returned from wherever it was that they had been. The lesbians were sympathetic but remarkably placid considering how fond they professed to be of me. In fact, I remember Gary once joking that they loved me more than he did. They had seen no previous signals of what happened. "Don't worry," they said, "Gary is a proud and uncaring person." They had seen him be indifferent and even cruel before. They said he is vain and has little patience for crying, which to him is ugly. Once again, this was interesting commentary from "best friends." My other friends sympathized and went through the breakup-comforting playbook.

The problem was I was dealing with much more than a breakup: a total breakdown. I had been thrown in so many emotional directions so quickly, and my life was completely without a center. I had lived in three different cities in less than a year and traveled nonstop for nearly five. I had no hobbies or regular activities, no friends I consistently saw or spoke with. I worked eighty hours a week on frequently changing projects, and I was completely done with my job. My health was constantly being buffeted by some new random ailment. Nearly every new relationship I made socially—romantic or not—ended in some kind of break, often a dramatic one. My friend had slowly died before my very eyes, and I had been barely there for her. My heart had been broken twice in one year, and the two separate futures I had looked toward snatched away. I was spent: out of ideas, out of energy, and suffering intensely. There was not a single positive thing I could think of to say for myself and not a soul I knew who loved me. All I could do was cry, which I probably did dozens of times a day, especially once my project ended, and I wasn't working regularly.

The festivities continued on Gary's Facebook profile—a surf trip to Bali and seemingly daily partying, with some hints of a little romance. I couldn't take it anymore and defriended him. I would not want to be friends with someone who did not have any emotional reaction to the breakup of a serious relationship or empathy or concern for his former partner, who was suffering. Each jubilation was a mockery of my pain. In my mania, at least, I knew enough to stay far away from him.

Chapter 9 - Life or death

My foot surgery was scheduled for the beginning of November, when the infected portions of my foot were to be cut away, leaving me largely immobile for some weeks. So, my last treatment before the surgery occurred sometime in late October, and because these were getting progressively more painful, this one was excruciating. It occurred on a Saturday afternoon. I cannot remember what I did the rest of that weekend, but I undoubtedly was hobbling around alone at home. Weight was peeling off of my body because I was not eating, and I went days without sleeping. On Sunday evening Oliver contacted me. His schedule was typically pretty flexible, and Monday was his day off. He wanted to see me, especially when I explained my condition to him. I told him I wasn't in the mood to see anyone, and he played a cutesy game that I was rejecting him. So, I agreed to see him the next day. He said he'd come over and bring me lunch.

The next morning the day stumbled into my room after a sleepless, frenzied night of what had become the usual tossing and turning, crying and wondering what the hell I was doing alive and where I was going. I knew I had to get out of the house, so I got dressed for work, even though I had no project going on and typically took the liberty of avoiding the office on such days. I remember standing somewhere in the middle of my room trying to button my shirt and just not being able to do so. It was like one of those dreams in which you are trying to perform a very simple task to escape the jaws of a fierce monster, but for some unknown reason cannot manage to do so, even in defense of your own life. I was moving in slow motion with dulled senses, like going snorkeling without fins.

I stepped out into the alley, and the sun hurt. I walked in the shadows to the subway station, conveniently located just beneath Gary's house. At the office, with nothing to do, I pushed papers around and added my two cents to emails where I was just on the CC list and really had little stake. I went to the bathroom frequently and broke down a few times before even reaching the stall. On my way to the pantry, one of the administrative staff asked me to come into her office. She asked me to take a seat, and she said she had spoken with some of her colleagues, and they were worried about me. I looked sick and exhausted. I had lost weight. Shouldn't I just take some time off? Did I need to go home to my family? What could she do to help? I needed to get out of there. I felt like I was sensing the first trembling of an earthquake and looking for a safe place to hide. Telling her whatever I told her to ease her concern, I limped over to my desk and grabbed my belongings. The shaking grew more violent, and my panic rose.

When I reached the elevator lobby, the doorman was holding the door as usual. I got out of there as fast as I could in my condition, without causing a scene, and I leaned up against the exterior wall, taking deep breaths. I was Indiana Jones having just run out of the collapsing cave, huffing and puffing, energy spent. But unlike Indiana so many times, I was not running into triumph with a damsel in tow, instead greeting my mortal enemy right in the eye, which for me was...my life. It was a beautiful day, but what was I going to do? I texted Oliver. When was he coming with lunch? I was ready. I reached home before I got his response. He had procrastinated the night before and not gotten his work done. He had some things to do. Maybe we could do a late lunch.

Late lunch time came and went, and he got back to me again saying that he was still caught up and would be over before dinner. He would bring me something because walking was proving increasingly painful with each step. Sheer exhaustion of not having slept properly in days plus coming down from that morning's adrenaline rush overcame me, and I passed out on my sofa.

It was raining when I woke up. The red alert light on my black-berry was blinking like the searching eye of a Cyclops. A message from Oliver: It's raining, too much trouble to travel now, maybe over for a late dinner. I was nearly hysterical. I was starving at this point, and my foot was in terrible pain. I told him so, and he responded not to worry—he'd be over later. It must have been around eight o'clock when he dropped the news on me, nonchalantly as could be. Never mind—he was too distracted by his work and wouldn't be coming. I could not dissemble any longer, and my next message was very blunt. It went something like this: "Oliver, I cannot remember my last meal, and my exhaustion along with the pain in my foot means if you don't come, I don't eat today. You know I am not in good shape." I still remember his flippant response. "Oh hahaha, you'll be fine!" With that, the curtain came down—I was alone.

The crossover of one day to the next failed to make any impression on me, and at some point the next morning I was lying on the floor, staring into my laptop screen. I had pills on my mind. So many pills from years of illness—muscle relaxants and strong pain killers for my back, migraine medication, steroids for my lungs, sleeping pills. It would be so easy to swallow all of those pills. When I was a child, my first time trying to swallow a pill was a seasickness capsule prior to a whale watch we were going on as a family. My parents tried burying it in jelly, putting it on my tongue, and making me drink, but nothing worked. Somehow it eventually went down, but it was a long and painful process. Years later in high school, when I needed to take a pill for something, a friend's grandfather suddenly grabbed my nose, and the pill slid down effortlessly. That was the trick—just hold your breath. Ever since, I have been able to swallow any size of pill without water. It would be so easy. I could swallow all of the pills without a problem!

But why was it, I wondered, if this were such an easy task, did so many people fail? There must be a reason. So, I Googled it and found the answer. After a certain point, most people's gag reflex takes over, and they vomit up the pills. The trick was to also take an antivomiting medication to make sure the medication stays safely in the digestive track, where it can be absorbed into the blood. Easy.

I got dressed and went into town. I would tell the pharmacist that I needed the antivomiting medication, because that should be something they can give without a doctor's visit. What if she didn't believe me? I had a backup plan if the first pharmacist refused to give me the medication. Before going to a second nearby pharmacy, I was going to go into the bathroom and induce myself to vomit. She would smell it on my breath, so there was no way she could deny me. As I walked into the pharmacy, another complication arose in my mind. So, I would tell her I was vomiting, but why? Did I have the flu, a hangover, a stomach ailment? My answer would certainly influence her decision on whether to give me the medication. What would I tell her? Why did I want this medication?

I wanted it so I could kill myself. I wanted it so I could just make the pain go away already. As I said that to myself clearly and without qualification, my steps slowed, and I paused, turned around, and left the pharmacy. My panic and mania had been gathering steam, preventing me from sleeping, inducing me to dress myself and come all this way. The nervous energy that shook my body and made my thoughts swim for days had finally coalesced into a force that drove me toward this purpose. And yet, right before I could close the deal, I stopped. Why? This seemed to be the first thing in weeks I could screw myself up to accomplish, and at the last moment, I had failed—I chose life.

I dragged myself home and went to sleep, stopping on the way for an ice cream cone.

Chapter 10 - Getting back on my feet

I slept all day and woke up in the evening, going another day more or less without food. When I awoke, the deep depression that had settled in me remained, but the nervous energy that had shaken my body for days was gone. I was not exhausted but rather just extremely low energy. My head, however, was clear. For the first time in weeks, I could think clearly, without the thoughts jumping one over another, all screaming for my attention.

I knew I needed help. I had just tried to end my life. I would be headed into a gruesome surgery that would see portions of flesh on my foot removed, with a recovery time of a month at minimum. My clothes were hanging off of me, I could not sleep, apart from when I collapsed out of sheer exhaustion. There was almost no one I could turn to for companionship and nothing I could do other than work, which I detested, I had nothing to occupy my body or my mind, which was still very much involved in ruminating over the past.

The next few weeks ahead of my annual Thanksgiving trip back home the US were easier and more difficult. On one hand, I found a few rare friends who seemed to care, some of whom I had not spent much time with in the past several years. Chief among these were the gay couple who had taken me in prior to my time in Paris. When I explained to them my situation, that I could no longer be alone and would certainly physically need help after my surgery, they agreed to take me in until I was okay to be by myself. Once my permanent transfer date to Hong Kong at the end of February was set, this period would certainly last the rest of my time in Singapore. I knew I would be gone on business most of January and February, after a long trip to New Zealand I would take for Christmas and the New Year in lieu of the previous plans in Tanzania. Besides my hosts, I met up with a few people I had once known well before disappearing into the black hole of my work and relationship with Peter. Each of them showed a concern and genuine empathy that I had not seen or felt in years. Whereas I had felt so alone since my time with Peter, suddenly I felt some kind of connection and was comforted. I even made a new friend from work, someone who had previously just been an acquaintance. She now came over from time to time to see me. The lesbians met with me once again and also had little to say other than their criticisms of their best friend Gary, but they went silent after my surgery and I never heard back from them again.

On the other hand, that I could now think in a clear and linear fashion led to hours-long stretches of rumination. After I had my surgery, my foot was bleeding constantly, and my bandages needed to be changed many times a day, so I spent a lot of time immobile, alone with my thoughts. How had I arrived to this point? Gary actually had not done anything wrong to me—he was the most caring and generous a person had ever been to me when we were in a relationship. When he no longer cared for me he was honest and did not waste my time in the way Peter had. So why did I want to cut off all relations with him? Why was I so revolted by his behavior? Even if I could confront him in an imaginary court in my head, of what would I accuse him? And, what did his behavior say about me? Indeed, what did Peter's behavior and my five years of floundering with very little to show for it say about me? More important, what was I going to do now? Why would anything be different in Hong Kong or anywhere else? Hopelessness, a deliberate, rational hopelessness, set in. Manic depression turned into just plain old depression.

I was low energy and globally negative, and though better than before, my appetite was very weak, and I was unable to sleep more than a few hours at a time. However, as my mind spun its wheels, it did turn out some cogent and rational answers. I realized pretty quickly how I had fallen so low. I had given everything up, and as my life became devoid of passions and hobbies and friends—connection, in a word—I had increasingly put all my self-worth into my relationships. My happiness depended on Peter and then Gary's happiness. If the relationship was stable, I was successful. If it was on the rocks, so was I. I had lost all passion for life, and hence had complied with whatever Peter and Gary wanted. I had lost all contact with the universe other than the one link my love of those two people provided in succession. Although I didn't know why I had allowed this to happen or what it might mean for the future, the most important thing was plain enough: if I was to survive, I would need to start rebuilding my life independently piece-by-piece. In that sense, going to a new place would probably be very helpful indeed.

The second piece that became clear rather quickly over just a couple of weeks was about Gary and his behavior. Though extreme, his behavior and attitude became more comprehensible when considering his background, which was nothing if not extreme. All those years, brutalized as a child, facing constant insecurity, everything and everyone seemed to betray Gary. He became hardened, and his cutting off of people, his refusal to recognize or accept suffering, was simply his defense mechanism. He refused attachment because of all the broken attachments. He had been so abused by the world but rarely had been the recipient of any empathy and hence thought little of empathizing with others. And yet, through all of those years, his rock and salvation had been his family. Everyone needs to love and to trust and to give. For Gary, his only outlet for love, his only deep human connection had been his family.

This was the driving force behind his obsession with having a perfectly provided for, showcase family: this was the only way he could imagine to integrate and perpetuate love in his daily life. When I became part of that vision, he nurtured and cared for me in the way that his family had done for him. As soon as I was out of the family picture, I was as useless, expendable, and unreliable to him as everyone else. He had no desire to feel or understand what I was going through because he did not allow himself to feel responsibility or sadness for other people. Myself, his best friends whom he thought stupid or spoiled or something worse, the woman who cleaned the toilets in his office—we were all part of that cruel, scary, and turbulent world, and

Gary's means of protection was to cut himself off emotionally. The only people to be truly let in were family, and other people could be fun to drink with or joke with or sleep with, but they were to be kept at an arm's length, and if there was any negativity surrounding the relationship, then they were cut.

It was a tragic story, but it also made a lot of sense. My emotions were mixed. As a hyperlogical and overly analytical person, putting the pieces together calmed my mind down a little. Although I felt a little better in knowing that the breakup was not due to any deficiency in me per se, it did, however, raise a scary question: How messed up was I that I had allowed my very sense of self-worth to hang on someone who was so clearly emotionally disturbed? Fairly early on in our relationship I had indeed recognized the scars that Gary's traumatic life had left on him, so why had I not extricated myself from the situation? Furthermore, my comprehension of the situation did nothing to allay the more operative concern: Why had I let myself get to that place, and how could I build a healthier, happier and more hopeful future? What indeed was wrong with me?

Only barely functioning and very obviously depressed, I finally decided I needed some professional help, and for the first time ever saw a therapist. It was mid-November. She was a kindly, peaceful, and motherly figure, unlike all like the fierce New York Jewish and Italian mothers I had grown up around. She made me feel a little better just being in her presence. During my months with her, she helped me work through a lot, but her earliest and perhaps most helpful contribution to my healing process was to help me deal with the guilt of being depressed. Like many people, I felt ashamed to have felt that way, especially when many people had been through much worse things and pulled through alright. She introduced me to Holmes and Rahe's Social Readjustment Rating Scale (SRRS), which scores stressful events in people's lives over the last year and gives them an overall stress score. A score of 300+ indicates the highest risk of becoming ill in the near future, though the illness would not necessarily be depression.

Although we had to take some liberties in calculating my score (for instance, accounting for separation of a mate vs. a spouse, and so on), my score was well over 400. According to my therapist, I was likely undergoing a "massive depressive episode," and she encouraged me to see a psychiatrist in addition to her treatment. It was actually a big relief. I knew at least what was likely wrong with me medically as well as the medical justification for that, based on years of research. In fact, the study said I had greater than an eighty percent chance of suffering a stress-related illness. No wonder I was depressed!

The psychiatrist gave me the official medical diagnosis and put me on a cocktail of antidepressant, anti-anxiety, and sleep medications. This was also a scary step for me, because I had never imagined needing to take drugs for this type of problem, but at this point I was just barely making it through the day and knew I needed help. The drugs did help me become a functioning person again, with more normal sleep cycles and a healthier appetite. The medications also affected an important physical change in me. Before, I had felt as if a great weight were sitting on top of my head, hunching me over and slowing me down both physically and mentally. Luckily I was out of work at this time because I had difficulty performing even relatively simple tasks and had no attention span whatsoever. The medication seemed to lighten me up and allowed me to engage in normal conversation. Though crying was still at least a thrice-daily activity, I could get through hours-long dry stretches.

My condition was thus when I went home to New York for my usual Thanksgiving week with the family. My family and close friends could tell there was something wrong, which I just explained as being a little run down from work and illness. I cried through the Broadway production of *Wicked*, which I had wanted to see for years, even though I was in the company of a dear friend I hadn't seen in some time. I did my best to distract myself with family and old friends, but it was clear that I was not connecting. My mind was still fixated on all of the questions and all of the emotions.

One positive outcome of my trip was that my overly analytical, hyperlogical side did actually receive a lot of closure on the question of

Gary. While I was away, one fair-weather friend—one of the ones who had disappeared on me—suddenly contacted me to ask what had happened between Gary and me. I was surprised, not knowing that this person was even aware that Gary and I ever dated or even knew each other! Why did he want to know, I asked. He said that one of his good friends and Gary were now seriously dating. "Since when?" I inquired. Oh, for a month or so. Doing the math in my head, that would place the beginning of their relationship not two or three weeks after Gary ended it with me, similar to how Gary began pursuing me not a month after his previous relationship ended. My 'friend' was not concerned for me at all when I told him what happened but was merely fishing for information. I was happy to oblige because what he told me qualified as more than a fair trade.

Intrigued, I did a little Facebook stalking, and what I found could not have fit the narrative more perfectly. The two had already traveled together, and there were silly little pictures of their feet, of walks on the beach, naps at home, little love notes on each other's profile walls. It was a perfect replay of our relationship—a lot of cloying sugary sweetness and a high degree of commitment (as evidenced by international travel so early on) very quickly. Indeed, Gary's Facebook page resembled that of a devoted lover's shrine to his soulmate. I was only a little startled not to have seen pictures with Gary's family already. It was a little creepy.

Contrary to what might have been expected, this did not upset me at all because it absolutely confirmed what I had thought about him. He was just looking for a person to be the new family member in his life, and he did everything to inflame his passion and convince himself that he had found that person. Furthermore, contrary to his earlier comments about taking some time off to think about how his feelings toward me had soured so quickly, he had jumped into a relationship immediately, without any apparent hesitation, and I would guess little self-reflection. If he were to tire of this new person just as quickly, so what? I remembered what he had said, that he does not care how what he does impacts other people and does not take responsibility for the consequences of his actions. If the new guy were to get hurt, well then Gary was just teaching him a lesson, right?

The only thing left to do was speak to Gary directly to get the final confirmation of my suspicions, which I did the day I returned to Singapore. Our last communication, weeks before, prior to defriending him, had been amicable, so the call should not have been too out of the ordinary. I called from an office line he would not have recognized, and as soon as he heard it was me, his voice turned to ice. "What do you want?" he seethed.

"Oh nothing—just to catch up. After all, we ended it as friends, so what's so odd about that?

"We might have been, but not anymore!"

"Well why not?"

First, it turned out that the lesbians had been reporting to him as soon as I reached out to them, and whatever they told him had been at best partial truth, because it had been them badmouthing him, not me. In my extreme pain and confusion at that time, I just had wanted comforting and some answers. Whatever they told him, however, must have angered him greatly. Furthermore, Gary was angry at my even remaining in contact with them. When I reminded him that I had even given them the key to my house to stay there while I was traveling for business and their house was being renovated, he said: "They didn't even end up staying there, and don't confuse your kissing up to my friends with them being your friends!"

He also noted that I had defriended him on Facebook, which I explained easily—seeing the frequent postings of joyful images hurt me enormously, as I was suffering and felt worthless seeing his nonstop celebration. When he asked why it was odd that he was celebrating, I stated the obvious: "That's not normally a person's reaction to pain or the breaking of a significant relationship."

What he said again struck me for reasons I only understood much later: "Did it ever occur to you that because of my background I don't react to things like other people do? I don't feel pain at other people's loss because I've had enough of my own, and I just move past the garbage in my way. You just have to deal with it however you want. I really don't care."

Again, this is certainly not a completely accurate quote, but it is the best I can remember and captures a lot of the specific language and certainly the essence of his comments.

Then, to give him one final chance to show me that I was wrong, to show even one iota of empathy or understanding, I recounted everything that had happened, including my own suicide attempt, the therapy, the medications—all of it. He listened in stony silence, though his rage silently pulsed through the phone. Having heard my tale, his reaction was merely this: "Are you done?" He had heard enough. Empathy, pity, regret, remorse—no thank you! No thread of whatever love or connection he had felt for me less than two months before remained. Love turned to hate while a new love bloomed for another, and it seemed not even a moment of introspection had occurred. I was glad to be far away from him at this point.

This completely satiated the logical side of me and left me feeling a lot better. I knew definitively that it was not me, it was him, and for sure that I was much better off without him. I was pleased that I had cut him off because this was indeed someone I would never want to associate with and found both tragic and frightening. That I had been with him was a sign of how far I had fallen. Even now, I recognize this as an important step in my recovery.

And yet, the triumph was short-lived. The sobbing spells returned, and the mind would not drop the matter. Something wanted to be found, but this time, instead of the voice inside my head formulating arguments, listing questions, and making plans, there was just a general and undefinable unease that transcended logic or articulation. It was another false start, and whereas I thought the matter was settled, it very soon took on another life form, all inside my head of course.

This coincided with my reading of a spiritual text passed to me by one of my friends in the US, to whom I had actually told the entire story. The book dealt with spiritual concepts I had never much considered: being present, oneness, compassion, empathy, joy versus happiness, empathy versus sympathy. It took me a long time to get through the book because it was all new and seemed largely incomprehensible. And yet, something resonated. I realized perhaps the most dreadful feeling I had was one of being completely untethered, without any anchor of stability. I had been to dozens of countries in the last few years, gone through friends like laundry, and the only stable things I had were my relationships, both of which had ended in rejection. The book claimed that accepting the fact that life is inherently unstable is probably the most important secret, because, even if one arranges one's life to give a complete illusion of stability, stability is never really there. The perfect marriage? That can't really mean anything when people themselves are constantly changing. The perfect job? Eventually, you get promoted or fired, the company comes under new ownership—whatever. Perfect health? You're getting older every day, and someday a new epidemic may come along. Once you accept and relax into the constant flux of things, life becomes a lot lighter and less consequential. You can stop being so serious and start observing and just enjoying the changes as they come, admiring the variety and richness of life. By surrendering to this ever-changingness, you actually gain more effective control by focusing on what you actually can influence. This was an idea that made a lot of sense to me and gave me great comfort, because I had very few constants in my life.

Travel once again gave me a temporary reprieve. Having worked some hundred hours a week for the first two weeks in December, I was off to a two-week-plus adventure vacation in New Zealand. Although the prices were sky high by the time I booked, this was something I had always wanted to do. After years of living to please others—Peter and his enormous social circle, Gary, my bosses—I felt I owed it to myself to finally do something just for me. My foot was still bandaged and had open wounds, but I was determined, and on that trip I scaled mountains above the snowline, above the clouds. I swam the oceans and hiked the forests, all the while with the book in my bag. Though I had some painful moments due to my foot, and the random emotional outpourings continued, though less insistently, I finished the book and enjoyed the trip immensely. It was safe to say I was at least getting back on my feet.

Chapter 11 - Soaring

The left side of my brain was satisfied. At last everything made logical sense! My body was mostly healed, pending a follow-up sinus surgery I was scheduled to have in February. Work was miserable, but I was traveling to Hong Kong weekly, a place I loved and where I would be moving. My therapist was helping me, the medications were stabilizing my moods and bodily rhythms, though emotional meltdowns still occurred at least a couple of times a week. February would be largely work free, as my project would be over at the end of January, and I was to travel to Dubai for a company training, which would be more of a reward and retention plan than serious work. After that, I figured I would spend time in New York with my family to use up my extra vacation days, especially given how close Dubai is to New York (this perspective exhibits how out-of-hand my life had become). My final move to Hong Kong would come after that. So, though I still didn't really know how I was going to live in the future, I was falling back into the motion of life.

Something within, however—my right brain, my soul, my heart—was not satisfied. I had finished the spiritual book and had a voracious appetite to know more. With some of the down time I had in February, I began a reading spree that would continue for more than a year. Most of the books were of a spiritual nature, but I read widely. There were autobiographical books, psychology, what can loosely be described as self-help, career, goal-setting books—and fiction. Although not really learning any new information, I nevertheless found my perception expanding and my perspective on life changing. I was seeing the world and looking at my past and future with a new lens rather than thinking about everything analytically, as I had been wont to do. Here is my reading list during that time:

- Brené Brown, *The Gifts of Imperfection*
- Brené Brown, *Daring Greatly*
- Byron Katie, *I Need Your Love - Is That True?*
- Charles Duhigg, *The Power of Habit*
- David Sedaris, *Me Talk Pretty One Day*
- Eckhart Tolle, *A New Earth*
- Eckhart Tolle, *Stillness Speaks*
- Eckhart Tolle, *The Power of Now*
- Ellen Degeneres, *Seriously...I'm Kidding*
- Erich Fromm, *The Art of Loving*
- Gina Lake, *What About Now?*
- J. D. Salinger, *The Catcher in the Rye*
- Jill Bolte Taylor (Ph.D.), *My Stroke of Insight*
- Marci Alboher, *One Person / Multiple Careers*
- Mark Nepo, *The Exquisite Risk*
- Mark Nepo, *Finding Inner Courage*
- Maya Angelou's collected autobiographical novels
- Neil Pasricha, *The Book of Awesome*
- Paulo Coelho, *The Alchemist*
- Pema Chödrön, *Living Beautifully*
- Pema Chödrön, *Taking the Leap*
- Pema Chödrön, *When Things Fall Apart*
- Ram Dass, *Polishing the Mirror*
- Robert M. Sapolsky, *Why Zebras Don't Get Ulcers*
- Stuart Brown (M.D.), *Play - How It Shapes the Brain, Opens the Imagination and Invigorates the Soul*
- Tina Fey, *Bossypants*

What I now realize is that I was on a turbo-charged path of spiritual growth. Ram Dass explains an ancient teaching from India that asserts that there are three ways to acquire spiritual knowledge: (a) through experience (probably most common and very often some kind of emotional breakdown, as the lives of most of authors of the above books demonstrate), (b) through reading books, and (c) through a teacher, or someone who knows about it. Without knowing it, I was undergoing a powerful process whereby all of these methods were simultaneously supporting and referring to one another.

I had experienced a total breakdown in which everything I thought I was supposed to be and how life should turn out completely imploded. Though I realized this only in hindsight, my ego—all the stories I had told myself about who I was—had reached a tragic crescendo, and I stood on the threshold of death by my own hand. In that moment, all my failed plans and misfortunes, all the things all those people had done to me, all the things I had done to and told myself, had driven me to suicide. In the face of such hopelessness, that was really the only logical thing to do. And yet, I had survived—I hadn't gone through with the unthinkable. Somehow all of what had driven me to do it and the voice in my head that told me in cool logic that death was the only way to make the pain stop, had been mistaken. And very quickly, as I recovered, with help from my therapist, the medications, my adventure trip, my reading, some time off, and all of the rest of it, it seemed that those stories unraveled. Sure, everything that had happened, had happened—the events of my life, of course, were real. Yet, their effect on me had dissipated into thin air. The stories and the voice were somehow mistaken—or lying.

I felt weightless and invisible, floating towards who knew what, or more likely in no particular direction. Having been stripped of the illusions that had brought me to this place near death and with no clear idea of, or even preference for, where I was going other than Hong Kong, I was in a vulnerable yet remarkably vibrant place. I was like a ripe fruit with all of the outer layers of stuff having rotted and fallen off, leaving behind a seed. The seed is fragile—it can be tossed about in the breeze, trampled underfoot, eaten by animals, but, the seed breaks open and grows into something new. It is like a baby, so fragile and so in need of protection, yet in the stage of its life where it grows and learns the most, due in no small part to the fact that it has no preconceived notions, biases, accumulated pain, or grievances against the world. That's what my experiences did to me: they opened me up to the growth and change that were to come. Having almost died by believing a tragic story, I stopped believing it but didn't yet know what to think. Having stepped back from the threshold, what more was there to fear?

So, my experiences opened me. The books, some of which I have listed above, taught me. The spiritual ones talked directly about concepts I would have previously dismissed as nonsense, hocus pocus, or New Age blather: the ego, connectedness, surrender. The psychology and liberally defined self-help ones introduced other important themes like the power of vulnerability, the courage of authenticity, and the practice of gratitude and love—and provided some more tangible strategies to integrate these things into daily life. The autobiographical works and fictions provided inspiring examples and entertaining illustrations, adding some insights of their own. And that is what the books did: they flooded me with wisdom, which I was now able to receive, my smugness and viewpoints having been washed away by the pain of my experience.

The surprising part was the teachers. My teachers were not paragons of the virtues, values, lessons, and teachings I was digesting from the books but rather a series of antiteachers who largely exhibited or even extolled the opposite of what I was reading. Chief among these: Gary. Remaining a hyperlogical and linear thinker, it was extremely helpful for me to see real, tangible examples that brought to life the wisdom from the books. Being such an extreme person as the result of some extreme experiences, Gary provided stark and unmistakable illustrations of what not to do.

For example, one of the very basic concepts behind all of the spiritual texts I was reading was the ego, the identity we create for ourselves based on all of our past experiences, often negative ones. This identity is the result of our fear of change and represents the very essence of the original sin—people's fight to keep things stable when all is change. The ego is our attempt to hold ourselves stable in world of flux and therefore becomes the lens through which we interpret the world, the pillar of our stable worldview. If we can't keep anything constant, we tell ourselves, at least we can define ourselves. From our stable vantage point, we shut off the constant change that is life itself, and we never really know the world around us, only our ego-projected interpretation of it. We are also blocked from the people closest to us, who are in a state of constant change. We never really know them either, but rather our own filtered view of them that hardens into self-projected prejudgment of their motivations, character, and worthiness. And, without really opening ourselves to people without the wall of who we judge them to be, we can't truly empathize with them either. So, the ego obscures true compassion as well.

And this from Gary: "With all that I've been through, I've learned what a hard and terrible place this world is…I've learned to be strong…You have to be strong in this world to achieve things, and you have to just not care who gets hurt along the way." So, his pain and fear had taught him to be a tough person in the cruel world, which is how he defined himself. This toughness required him to hurt other people as a defense mechanism and not care about it: quite the opposite of living with empathy, compassion, the notion of connectedness, and responsibility. And, this toughness was a tool to achieve things, without which I suppose life is meaningless in Gary's view. Gary's many such statements to me were so opposed to everything I was reading, and his life story and treatment of me provided living examples of the dynamics of a nonspiritual, or rather antispiritual life. His past provided the tragic causes, his actions the consequences, and his view of the world, so clearly articulated as to become a sort of manifesto, was the dark logic that tied it all together. This is just one basic example—there are many others.

The process—me being open as a result of my breakdown, receiving wisdom from books, and seeing from Gary's example of what happened when that wisdom was rejected or unknown —could have ended there, and it would have been a useful process. What made it a transformative one, however, was that my smugness and self-satisfaction were gone. My ego, how I saw myself, and the stories I had convinced myself of, had largely melted away. So, whereas my previous instinct would have been to rationalize my actions or defend myself in the face of these new perspectives, now I was curious to inquire. How did all of these concepts show up in my life until now, and how did I live them?

What I found startled and horrified me, but it was the logical and indispensable conclusion of this now three-part process: read and learn, see the wrongness very clearly in Gary, and then see the wrongness, typically in more subtle ways, in myself. It had suddenly become painfully obvious to me how my youthful experiences, which I have recounted above, had made me into the person I thought myself: always fighting to get the attention of my parents and always on the losing end of any altercation with one of my more favored siblings. I had learned to be tough and showy and arrogant. My alpha male-ness drive to achieve was largely fueled by the need to garner the attention and approval I had so sorely missed as a child, and the tough exterior I put on at work and elsewhere was my attempt to dissuade people from messing with me. In my years of playing this role, all driven by my accumulated pain, how many people had I hurt or offended or missed entirely? How much opposition had I engendered in others, who therefore reacted to the ego I was play-acting, shutting off our potential mutual relationship? And, when they reacted badly, this had only strengthened my tough exterior and hardened my resolve to be alpha. Thus my ego perpetuated itself. How much time had I wasted in prestigious jobs meant to impress rather than pursuing my real passions? So, while I was nowhere near as malevolent and extreme as Gary, the life experiences that had led to my unconsciousness were also much less dramatic than his had been. Nevertheless, my ego had defined and limited my life experiences in the same way his had and caused me often to be a petty, unimaginative, and sometimes cruel.

So that was the process: I read, I saw an extreme example of what I had read in Gary (or sometimes Peter or one of the other characters who had come into my life story), then I saw it in myself, and then I made a commitment to change, doing my best to find daily practices to institutionalize the change. This iterative process brought forth a rapid transformation in me by simultaneously incorporating all three elements Ram Dass had cited.

I finally moved to Hong Kong in March of 2013, and despite walking into an even more stressful working environment than I had been surrounded with in Singapore and being required to undertake an equal amount of travel—in a year my life changed. The difference was that now, for the first time, I drove a lot of the change. The depression and rumination slowly tapered off. I finally transformed my work to something I cared a lot more about and that allowed me time to pursue my passions. I pared down my social circle to invest in the most high-quality relationships. And, somehow, I dropped the alpha-male persona.

Beyond all these outward shifts, however, obvious to anyone who knew me, the fundamental transformation had occurred within the way I reacted to the events around me, my attitude towards life, what I knew and knew I didn't know, and how I felt about it all. I relaxed and stopped taking things so seriously. Seemingly every day the process bore a new fruit: in daily moments of clarity, I saw something new and realized how I could make my life better by incorporating that something into my behavior and thought processes. The learning, growing, and changing continues to this day, albeit at an understandably more gradual pace. I arrived in Hong Kong just barely standing, but this process has allowed me to soar, gliding mostly peacefully through the turbulence of daily life and finding joy in what I would have previously seen as life's problems.

That is what this book is really about—the standouts from the thousands of little lessons I learned during this time and how they brought me out of the pain I had been suffering.

Part II. The Footprints Through the Desert

Introduction

None of what I am writing is meant to be new per se, nor is it an attempt to thoroughly explain or rehash the lessons of thousands of years of spiritual or philosophical writing by people much more well studied and enlightened than I. What I am attempting to do is chronicle the most important realizations I had, all of which have a basis in spiritual or some other literature. My story brought these lessons to life for me and opened me up to them. Whereas some could read an ancient esoteric religious text that really speaks to them and others might be equally moved by poetry or fiction, what I hope is that some can relate to my story and find truths in it. Indeed, even if one person's perspective is broadened by my tale, I will feel deeply satisfied.

Chapter 12: The only constant is change

The ultimate source of most emotional suffering in life—longing, pain, regret—is the refusal to accept that all life is change. We miss a person who is gone or a situation that is no more. We mourn who we were, what we lost, or a stillborn dream that never came to fruition. We hold onto something, anything, to provide a constant in our life, an anchor to keep us steady in the unceasing storm. This is the most fundamental mistake that will cause endless suffering in life.

The truth is that there are no anchors. You try to make the perfect marriage, because at least you'll always have that person—no matter what. Except you won't. That person you know today won't be the same person tomorrow. He or she will be changed by the wisdom or folly of experience, his or her body will be bent by age, weakened by illness, or strengthened by exercise. He or she may divorce you. He or she may get struck down by lightning.

You won't be same either. And then what happens once that seeming anchor is cut loose? You suffer at least in proportion to the degree that you had trusted and depended on that anchor.

The original and most fundamental anchor is, of course, the ego, which is literally who you are, or at least who you *think* you are. For instance, my ego sense was one of an alpha male because that's how my childhood had taught me to win approval and protect myself from mean people. Gary's separative ego sense was one of a wounded heart that sealed itself off from the dangers of compassion and empathy because he felt his past had amply fulfilled his quota of sadness and that the only way to avoid pain was not to relate too deeply with other people.

All of my strutting around had led me to make career choices that kept me from the people and activities that I loved and caused so many of my colleagues to see me as an arrogant and aggressive person. Their reaction only convinced me more of my need to be tough and ratcheted up my ego's response even further, thereby strengthening its hold on me. Every little failure or criticism was not a learning opportunity but an assault on my personhood or proof that the other parties didn't like me. I just had to try harder and be harder. The ways in which I suffered and the opportunities I lost because of this ego are innumerable.

Gary, similarly, in staunchly avoiding the pain of his past, perpetuated that pain for himself and others.

By definition, change involves a loss of something and a gain in something else. For example, you may lose a spouse or a child you dearly loved and cherished. Naturally, you experience extreme pain and sadness at the loss. As painful as it is, however, the loss of that child and the future you had in mind by definition opens up your time and your heart to new people, places, and possibilities. If that person has become an anchor, however—something you need in your life that cannot change—you are cut off from any recovery because your mourning—a very natural, real, and necessary thing—becomes perpetual. You experience only the loss and not the gain. You are cut off from gratitude for that person's part in your life because you can see only the loss. The sad truth is that had that person, your anchor, survived, you would have eventually lost your anchor anyway, causing more pain. The overbearing parent sculpting the perfect child becomes embittered when the little angel grows up, makes mistakes, no longer needs mommy and daddy, finds a mate—or dies. Life is change, and there are no anchors.

Dreams and goals can become another of these pernicious anchors. When playing a constructive role in life, they guide our love and passions into purposeful action to accomplish something important to us. However, almost everyone also falls into the trap whereby a goal becomes the Promised Land, the journey becomes a path of suffering. Not reaching the Promised Land is a failure to be mourned and regretted, another cause for recrimination of ourselves, of the bad people who stood in our way, of Fate, or of God. The doing—the journey itself—merely becomes a means to an end, a tedious or even miserable slog through the muck: "No pain, no gain," as the saying goes. One of the many problems with this view of life is that the journey comprises most of our time in this world, and to view it as a chore is to reduce life and its infinite possibilities to drudgery.

The irony is that on one of those rare occasions when we reach the Promised Land—when we get what we want exactly as we want it—the joy is often short-lived. The journey has changed us, or our grim determination has made us jaded and cynical, so maybe we find that we actually don't want the Promised Land so much anymore. Or, as quickly as we reach the place, it proves to be a mirage, because, like everything else, it too changes. You finally get that coveted manager role after years of misery at the company, rising through the ranks. Then, when you get it, you find most of your time is actually spent on administrative matters rather than the skill or trade of your previous line job. Or, the industry changes, and hence the job also. Maybe the company goes out of business, or you aren't all that great a manager and get fired. Then what? You have failed, suffered all of that time for nothing. Maybe that feeds into your ego, and you are the tragic character with all the bad luck who no one ever appreciates.

The funny thing is that the best things in life are indeed not what we intended. The ultimate example for me is my breakdown. An episode of massive depression and near suicide is something I never would have wished upon myself, but this led me to a make changes in my life that have brought me so much joy and taught me all of the most important things I now know. Conversely, think of what would have happened had I achieved my dream of Gary moving to Hong Kong with me and the two of us starting a family. What would have been the result of that? Maybe once he revealed his true colors we would have had a long, messy, and even more painful process in unwinding shared assets or shared children. Or, maybe I would have woken up one day and realized I had committed myself to a life with a sociopath.

In a more general sense, think of what life would be like if everything had turned out as you planned. That would indeed be a boring and terrible existence. Life would be stripped of all of its mysteries and possibilities. The truth can be so much greater than what the human imagination is capable of producing. I think of some of the places I have been: the majestic Pyramids of Giza, the barren plains of Tibet, the snow-frosted fells of Lapland, or the emerald and sapphire lakes of Jiuzhaigou. Having spent months planning, I arrive there, and it's more beautiful, more wild, more alive than what all of the planning, reading, and researching I had done could have conjured up in my mind. What inflexible anchor goals do to us is to reduce our lives to a slog and shut us off from outcomes so amazing we can't even imagine them. What is the worst thing that could ever happen to you? Death. What is the best thing that could ever happen to you? No matter the answer, you can think of something better.

I had numerous anchors in my life during these five or six miserable years I described above. They all fell away: my ability to achieve, my near-perfect record of health, my looks, my sense of home. As these illusions crumbled, I held more tightly to my relationships, which were for a time the one stable thing in my life. When, however, those failed, the only anchor left was my ego, the story of my life and who I was. The ego is always the star in one's own mind-made drama, and mine was the smart and successful alpha male who no one could get close to but was really a loving and caring person. All he needed and all he had was his partner: the only one for whom he would lower his defenses. He needed his partner to protect him from life's hardships, and his partner needed him, and they lived happily ever after. For me, when all of this failed I was ready to die. But I survived. The story was therefore proven false, and I finally cut off the anchor. It was only when this happened that I truly flourished and found joy in life.

So, what does life look like without anchors? Without a doubt, it is frightening when viewed from afar, and it will be so if one holds fast to the idea that life without anchors is frightening. When you tell yourself and are constantly reminded by society that you are supposed to be married and have kids, otherwise you aren't leaving anything behind, will die alone, and will have lived a selfish and inconsequential life, then of course a life without marriage and/or children becomes frightening. But, if you drop that thought and daydream a little, isn't it easy to picture a superconsequential, exciting, impactful, and love-filled life without forming a family? The possibilities are endless: you can become a yogi in India, you can start a charity in Africa, be a socialite in Manhattan, or become an environmental researcher in Antarctica. Of course, those are just some extreme examples—the permutations of a beautiful life are endless. In fact, it is only when you liberate yourself from the smallness of your mind—which conceives of all of these so-called must-haves—that you are truly free. Indeed, what is the purpose of an anchor? It stabilizes but prevents movement. Without it, you can sail wherever the horizon ends if you're brave enough.

When you want and appreciate things—a family, your health, the person you love— without defining those things as anchors, things you *need* or *can't live without*, you enjoy them more. You enjoy the challenges it takes to achieve them and—free from the fear of losing them—you love and enjoy their presence. That fear will at least make you unable to fully enjoy that thing because you are often caught up imagining losing it, but at times it will make you angry or vicious, like a cornered animal defending its life. In fact, that is exactly what you are defending. Your ego is what you perceive as the very meaning of your life, and your anchor becomes an integral part of who you are. The smallness of your mind tells you that without your anchor you are less or maybe even cannot exist.

In my own case, as my life became constricted to my sixteen-hour work days and my time with Peter, those became the two anchors in my life. I needed to succeed in my prestigious and demanding job. I needed to be successful because even if I had no real friends or hobbies and did nothing to make this world a better place, at least I would be admired, and the bad people wouldn't mess with me. I needed to make Peter happy because he was my one human connection, and without him there would be no one for me to love, and no one would love me. When I lost Peter, I needed to find a new person, and Gary was such an appropriate choice because he would vindicate my suffering. He was strikingly good looking, successful, exotic, and interesting. We had always been intrigued with one another. It was the storybook ending I needed.

Of course it was not an ending. There are no endings because life never stops. When I think back, much of my mind-space when I was with Gary was occupied by fear of losing him, plots of how to manipulate and lock him into our relationship, and thoughts of how I should make myself more appealing to him. This latter point served only to highlight what I saw as my inadequacies: making me a sadder or sometimes angrier person. When I lost him, there was nothing else to live for. I was totally out of ideas. And yet, I still breathed, revealing the fallacy of all of those discarded anchors to which I once held fast. How sick and backwards is all of that? I found the one thing I thought I needed constant, and it made me fearful and sad because I defined it as necessary for my personhood, an anchor to hold me stable in a turbulent world without which I would be adrift in a meaningless life. I was young, making more money than I could spend, traveling the world, and in love during my time with Peter and then Gary. It was a time that should have been light, fun, and exciting, but instead I saw it as a grim path of suffering to reach a desired end, without which I would have failed. Whereas an external observer would have seen a wonderful and successful life, I saw myself as a victim persevering though a cruel life's hail of slings and arrows. The anchors nearly drowned me.

My fear is that most people are not lucky enough to be struck by such a moment of clarity. Instead, the pain caused by their holding fast is a slow burn, as they grow gradually more afraid of the loss of their anchor, more determined not to let that happen, and more embittered that it is happening. What they cling to, which they see as the very fabric of their lives, is slipping through their fingers. So they pull tighter. However, the process typically does not reach such a dramatic moment of truth, and hence they hold on while life passes them by—unnoticed.

A life without anchors is movement. You float around in the rich heterogeneity of life, admiring the beauty, accepting the unpleasant things, and opening you heart to whatever happens because you know none of it will last. Change is constant. In this way, you are grateful every day for all the blessings in your life—your health, your friends, the weather—because all of it will change and eventually disappear, and there is nothing you can do to stop that. Contrast that to the bitter clinging as described above in which holding on to things makes us frightened of losing them and resentful of their often slow but inevitable loss. By accepting that life is change, you practice gratitude for the good and are thankful for fortune's visits to your life, which you actually notice a lot more because you are not laser focused on struggling to hold that anchor. As for the so-called bad or unpleasant things, you know they will not last forever, because life's endless currents will sweep them away also.

When you accept that life is change and that all anchors eventually fail, you can relax into the waves and currents of life as a skilled swimmer or surfer does. You realize that you can't hold on, so your energy and attention are less focused on defending, grasping, and clawing. You learn flow. Fear is replaced by the overflowing amusement, gratitude, and love that allowing the waves of ephemera to change brings. When you look into your lover's eyes, you don't get annoyed seeing the wrinkles age is inscribing around them, thinking about how to make him stay, mourning the loss of his youthful naiveté, or dreaming up all the scenarios that would cause you to lose him. Instead, you just look and love and say thank you for him and for this moment. Life becomes so much lighter, and you sit back and enjoy the ride without getting too caught up in the downturns, because those won't last either. You are thankful for what is but never try to own it or fall into the delusion that it is yours. Beauty is beauty—whether or not you are present to notice it.

However, if we are to accept change and relax into life, we certainly must accept what life throws our way—the blessings and the complications. This is the act of surrendering, or no longer fighting with life but figuring out how to work with it for the best outcome, all the while recognizing the boundaries over which we actually exercise control. Contrary to what many might believe upon reading this, surrender is not giving up on life, but giving up on *fighting* with life.

If one day someone is walking home through the woods and a flood comes and washes away the bridge across the river in his path, there are a number of options for purposeful action: backtracking and finding another path, calling for help, swimming across, building a new bridge, or raft, or even finding a new home on the available side of the river. All these require surrender, which is simply accepting that the bridge is gone and won't come back on its own. And, once one takes that positive action, one's life may change. One may learn a new skill in building the raft, get some exercise in swimming across, or make a new friend in backtracking along the path. Who knows what could happen? Most people, however, would not surrender. They would complain about the bridge being gone, damn the fates for their misfortune, or ponder what they did to deserve such bad luck. Not only does this entail emotional suffering, it actually delays or prevents them from taking the positive action that would have otherwise resolved the situation. Furthermore, because their emotions are still worked up and their nerves frayed, they will not be open to all of the possibilities with which they are presented. They will miss the beauty of the woodland scenery, will not appreciate the water's coolness, hear the birds' songs, or absorb the new skills they could learn from getting out of the predicament. When the love of their life walks down the path, they will be too absorbed in negative thought to notice her. In their frustrated haste, they may just trip over a root and split their lip open, causing even more suffering.

Far from the purposeless passivity that most people would associate with it, surrender is the key to taking positive and purposeful action and enjoying its fruits. When you no longer resist life and dwell on the emotions nurtured by that resistance, the scope of your attention narrows to what you can control: your reaction to the change life is presenting and your range of options to strengthen, mitigate, or tweak the change. Your ability to think clearly and influence the flow of life to your own desire is supplemented, not depleted, by the surrender.

In my own case, I was so focused on fighting with reality that I wasted years of my life in the wrong job and the wrong relationships and suffered the consequences: poor health from lack of sleep, constant fear of abandonment, poor self-esteem due to Peter's indifference, and unceasing criticism, devastation at having been rejected. If only I had accepted that my job was draining my energy and my life and that prestige was no longer doing it for me, I would have made the change, kept my health, and been able to enjoy the things I loved in life. If only I would have accepted the ways in which Peter's past had inhibited his ability to love and maintain an adult relationship, I would have come to a much clearer decision about what I was willing to accept and not been at the mercy of his fickle attentions. If only I would have accepted my realization of Gary's deeply troubled psyche and let go of my idyllic visions of our future together, I would have never been the victim of his emotional disability, which enabled him to leave me so suddenly alone again. And, last but not least, once I was left alone again, I dwelt on the cruelty and unfairness of it all and wallowed in a self-pity that nearly drove me to suicide. Of course, the whole time the beautiful world kept turning, and there were billions of people on earth lacking for much more than I was—food, water, shelter, and love.

None of this is to say I regret these past decisions, because they led me to this place along a path that endowed me with the tools I now have. In general, I no longer fight with life but accept change as it comes and don't torture myself with doomsday scenarios. I do complain when I need to vent, but when the complaining has allowed me to release whatever tension is in my mind and body, I end it there. I am so much more relaxed in my life, and most important, I am grateful every day for what I have, rather than bitterly dwelling on what was taken from me. This is surrendering to the change that is life and loving it.

I am, however, not asleep. Because my mind is clearer and less laden with the weight of fear and loss, I find I am more effective in my work and socially. And yes, I have faced loss and pain in the years since my recovery. I have cried and gotten hurt, but as with the complaints, I don't carry the tears or the pain very far with me, choosing instead to practice gratitude for the million things that are right rather than the one that is wrong (or was wrong when it happened but is no more, existing only as a thought in my mind). I love life without trying to own it. This is a life without anchors.

The cycle and the fallacy of pain

Pain is and isn't just like energy. According to the first law of thermodynamics, energy can neither be created nor destroyed but is merely converted from one form to another. The electrical energy that powers the pitching machine launches the ball, which has kinetic energy. The batter uses the chemical energy stored in his cells to swing the bat, the kinetic energy of which is transferred to the ball when it connects. Some of the bat's kinetic energy also becomes thermal energy when the two surfaces collide. The energy is just displaced from one object to another, but lives forever. You are in a sense harnessing the very energy of the sun when you lean out to open the window to let the sun shine in.

Pain is the same way, and the first law of pain is what I call the *cycle of pain*. The manager is belittled by his boss because the boss was frustrated with the latest quarterly results, which disappointed because the customers were unhappy with the product. Upset, the manager comes home and mouths off to his wife, who is carrying her own tribulations from work. The wife and mother then loses her temper with her son, who is hurt by his mother's outburst. In pain and having witnessed a bad example from his mother about what to do with frustration, the son then goes to school the next day and causes a fight in the classroom during the teacher's lesson. Her plans in tatters with the class disrupted, the teacher then exacts collective punishment on the whole class, who then each go and act out the negativity in their own separate ways. The cycle of pain never ends as the pain is transferred from one person to another in various forms. Anger can drive aggression in one person, which in turn becomes sadness or depression in another, which then causes worry from another. The form of the pain changes, but the pain doesn't go away.

Except it can. After all, pain differs from energy. First of all, pain can be created, added to, and multiplied or increased exponentially. Above, the frustration that the teacher caused can turn into sadness, hurt, or anger among her thirty pupils, who then have a negative emotional-energetic push to transfer and potentially increase the pain. More and more people are born and live longer each day, meaning there are more egos to feel and create pain. The internet and other mass communication technologies only expand each single person's ability to transfer and create more and more pain in more and more people. Weapons of mass destruction have the same function. This is a depressing picture.

The story, however, isn't all bad, and as conscious human beings we can actively work to stop the flow and creation of pain. When the husband comes home to vent at his wife, the wife can always ask what the matter is, listen compassionately, and react with love and a desire to help ease the pain. When the child acts out in school, the teacher can always take a deep breath, draw upon her compassion for whatever is driving an innocent child to be aggressive, pull the child aside, and try and find out what's wrong. If someone is aggressive and bullies or insults you, you can take a deep breath and recognize that the person is suffering in some way and needs to displace his or her pain through aggression. At that moment, you can give it right back to the person, which on a certain level of truth the person deserves, and you are "justified" in doing this. Or, you can store up the hurt and then transfer it to someone else later through your own passive-aggressive behavior, which makes you the aggressor and creates another victim. However, what you can also do is simply not react and instead be a sink—you let the pain pass through you, and then...it disappears. It's like water passing down a drain due to the natural force of gravity, without effort. Or even better, you can remember that this person is in pain and put your arm around him and ask how you can help, thereby maybe even creating a little gratitude.

If the analogy of a sink for pain doesn't work for you, an even more fitting but somewhat obscure analogy would be a salt marsh. Salt marshes are a natural habitat along coastlines. During storms, salt marshes absorb the force of large waves, which travel into the marshes, lose momentum, and dissipate. If they even hit the shore, the waves retain a fraction of their former strength, and the coast is thus protected. Sand dunes serve a similar function. Over time, people have degraded and destroyed these fragile habitats, making storms even more dangerous and destructive. To protect harbors, people have built sea walls made of stone. These walls appear strong, but actually sea walls can crumble with the force of being slammed by powerful waves or can even cause more destruction when waves ricocheting off of them create violent chop in the water. So, we can be like salt marshes or sand dunes. We can absorb the painful or destructive forces in the world and let them die with us. By throwing up walls and offering resistance, we will eventually break if a strong enough wave comes, or we will add to the pain of the world through our resistance. Unfortunately, telling someone to be a salt marsh or a sand dune might lack some of the rhetorical clarity of a pain sink. Pick your analogy.

So many people are drawn to the idea that they should do something to make the world a better place—run off to save some animal, feed the children, clean up the environment. Although all of those are worthy causes that need doing, think of how much better the world would be if every conscious person just made a simple commitment to be a pain sink, to let the pain pass through him or her and not to the next person. In the silly little example above, think of all the trivial tragedies that would have been avoided if even one person in the chain had made this decision. In an extreme example, but one based in reality, think of the disturbed person who might not have jumped off the building or pushed another person in front of the subway if someone had only offered a hand rather than huffing past the lunatic on the way to work. Pain destroys lives, and yet it can be so easy to dispel, if people were only conscious. We can all help protect the environment by not polluting it with our negativity. How much better would the world be if we all understood this to be our basic responsibility as loving beings?

The cycle of pain is so evident in all the main characters in my sad little story. Peter had grown up often with no father in the home, and when the father was home, the house was the scene of fighting, shouting, and physical punishment. At the same time, Peter was not encouraged academically, which further damaged his self-confidence as a child and drove him to poor academic achievement, which created an inferiority complex that stayed with him. A number of times in our relationship, Peter endeavored to humiliate me publicly. It took me quite a long time to uncover what was behind this because Peter was not comfortable expressing or examining his feelings, having never done so before. Finally, he came out with it: he felt overshadowed by my achievements and abilities, and he was trying to bring me down a notch. On those occasions, he and I fought and made the others around us uncomfortable, and I am sure they took that pain and put it somewhere else afterwards.

Even more important, driven into the shadows by the shame of homophobia, Peter acted out his repression similarly to many gay men, through having a wild, no-commitments, completely unbridled sex life. Into his thirties, when we met, Peter had never had a stable, committed, or monogamous relationship. As a result, over the years there were many dramas and many hurt people who I heard about. Peter's reaction was that he wanted sex and purposely didn't feel anything for these people, and if they wanted to play that game, they were responsible for their own emotional outcomes. On a certain level, our relationship must have been an incredible comfort and breath of fresh air for him. Here was someone who actually cared about him, was eager to hear his thoughts and opinions, and valued his advice. However, never far away were his well-established hedonistic tendencies, and he later admitted the obvious: that our relationship had been a terrible bore for him—another form of pain and negativity. This very well explains his constant criticisms of me and his withholding of intimacy, two things that made my self-worth sink lower and made me feel more and more desperate. In my desperation, I ignored and cut off friendships and people in need, and his eventual dumping of me caused such a depression that my work suffered, causing problems for my colleagues and my family and friends.

Gary presented an even starker illustration. Not only was his pain much more dramatic, but he was committed to it. He even acknowledged how it had shaped him and was devoted to the twisted virtue of not caring about people and even "helping" them by victimizing them.

Remember these chilling words: "I've learned what a hard and terrible place this world is. So, I do whatever I want to get what I want, and if I hurt someone else, that's really their own fault because they allowed it to happen to themselves. I've learned to be strong, and that's what I'm teaching them." Or, think about this one: "Did it ever occur to you that because of my background I don't react to things like other people do? I don't feel pain at other people's loss because I've had enough of my own, and I just move past the garbage in my way."

Though he claimed amorality, Gary had actually created his own moral code whereby he held fast to and honored his pain as a source of strength. Whenever it served his purposes, Gary was glad to hurt others, which, if the victims were clever would help convert them to his grim way of seeing humanity. The extreme pain of Gary's young life lived on as vividly as ever, and he passed it on to others like a gift. The cycle of pain was how Gary lived his life, like a kind of religion or guiding principle. Far beyond the normal unconscious pain pollution, this was a perverse devotion to hurting others.

My eventual understanding of the cycle of pain taught me one of the most critical lessons I will ever learn—those of forgiveness and compassion. Up until this difficult period in my life, I had always viewed forgiveness as something to be sought after and earned. If someone was trying to get it from me, they had to want it, show their contrition, and express some sort of indication of their intention not to wrong me in the same way again. Once again, there is a certain level of obvious truth to this sort of legalistic, justice-oriented definition of forgiveness. There is nothing wrong with this view per se, but as is often the case, there are also deeper layers of truth.

When viewed through the lens of the cycle of pain, one discovers that aggression, cheating, lying, bullying, violence, and other forms of hurting others are just different methods of transmitting and expressing pain. Through their life experiences, people acquire and store pain and either unconsciously, or from a deliberate acting out of learned coping mechanisms they unleash this pain on other people. In that sense, the one who passes the pain, as unjust as his or her actions might be, is suffering. Typically this is unconscious behavior: the person does not intend to do it. However, even for someone like Gary, who deliberately and knowingly goes out and hurts people, there is an unconsciousness to that behavior. If he wasn't suffering, he wouldn't need to hurt someone else, and even if he was suffering but was otherwise connected to and maintained healthy relationships with other people, he wouldn't do it either. In fact, his disconnection in itself is a form of suffering, and in a certain sense harming someone else can be a way of establishing a form of connection, however perverse. If Gary were truly conscious, he would realize that disconnection was causing his suffering and that by hurting someone else, he was prolonging his disconnection.

In this sense, despite your annoyance or surprise at someone else's unkind behavior, how can you begrudge him or her for it? Taking a theoretical example, suppose someone robbed you at gunpoint. Imagine this person was a single parent who had lost his or her job and was struggling to feed a family. Naturally, there would be a certain degree of understanding and empathy for the robber, given his or her desperation and the suffering that drove such an extreme act. How could you hate the person for doing what her or she did? How could you not recognize the person's suffering and forgive the person for it? As much as you are annoyed or repulsed by the crazy drunken man ranting and raving at you on the street corner, can you hate him? How can you not forgive someone who doesn't understand what he or she is doing? This is why our courts have a contingency for innocence based on insanity or lesser sentences based on extenuating circumstances.

Suddenly the words of Jesus Christ become a lot more tangible: "Love your enemies and pray for those who persecute you." Why pray for them? Pray for them because they are in pain, and just because they are trying to transmit that to you does not mean that you need to be in pain as a reaction to them. Be a pain sink and let it pass through you. It will disappear so long as you do not perpetrate that pain on yourself or someone else.

This truth also indicates another layer of truth, also expressed in the words of Jesus Christ. During his own execution, Jesus said of his executioners, "Forgive them, for they do not know what they are doing." The cycle of pain is a largely unconscious process, and even for those such as Gary who more or less consciously inflict pain on others, their actions are those of an insane person, even though they justify their behavior with a sort of logic.

Why is it insane? It is insane because human beings are born to connect. Connection with each other and the universe is what gives meaning to peoples' lives and sustains them through life's tribulations. Disconnection is at the root of loneliness, depression, and shame. To hurt someone else because you are hurting may displace the pain you feel, but the only way that happens is if you fail to recognize the connection between yourself and your victim. You do not know what you are doing. You cannot know what you are doing because if you did, you would realize you are either hurting yourself as well or cutting yourself off from your victim to block that pain. In either event, you will feel pain as a result, so both are insane.

So, you can see the insanity of the perpetrator, but why love him and why forgive him? Going back to our robber example above, imagine that it was actually a wealthy thief as opposed to a person in dire financial straits. The truth is that this robber may appear wealthy, but he is in fact impoverished no matter how much money he has. Beyond the obvious insanity that he is robbing someone for money he doesn't need, he also is doing so in spite of the pain he is causing the other person. He does not feel that pain and is in a state of disconnection. He has an impoverished life. He believes whatever story he has told himself about why he needs to victimize another person, and he either feels the pain of remorse or, like Gary, to block that pain cuts himself off from the victim. It is a life of poverty or scarcity.

What do we do to poor people? Do we hate them? No, we have compassion for them for the sorry state of their lives. Maybe they got there through their own reckless behavior, but they would not have done that if they had known what they were doing. And, to have compassion for or empathize with someone means you put yourself in that person's shoes: you identify with the unfortunate one. This is very different from sympathy or pity, both of which are the acts of objectifying people and feeling sorry for them. Even the greatest monster is capable of pity: a basic human instinct that requires neither responsibility nor commitment. When Hitler, for instance, saw the devastation wrought by the Allied bombing of German cities, can there be any doubt that he felt pity for the innocent victims of war? He was a human being, and those were the members of his own tribe. Why wouldn't he feel sorry for them? Empathy, however, would require him to feel the pain *with* the victims, evaluate his own responsibility in the matter, and consider his own human victims.

"Oh you poor thing, I feel so sorry for you!" Anyone can say those words and legitimately feel that sentiment. Compassion requires connection, and people hurting others either do not feel the pain and are therefore disconnected, or they enjoy the pain and are therefore insane. Therefore, we must have compassion for them.

At this point, forgiveness becomes a formality. It is automatic. Of course you forgive an insane person who doesn't know what he or she is doing. In this way, if understood intellectually and felt through one's connections with others, forgiveness becomes a state of being. At first glance, you might describe such a person living in forgiveness as unattainably saintly or completely selfless. However, one of life's great secrets is that forgiveness, in the words of Maya Angelou, is "one of the greatest gifts you can give yourself." The ability to let go of your anger or resentment at what all those people did to you—that is freedom. Words of wisdom from Hannah Arendt: "Forgiveness is the key to action and freedom." When you can forgive them, you free your attention, your emotions, and your energy to focus on your life and what you need to do. Once again, you can see the beauty of the world around you when you let go of your resentment, just as when you surrender and drop your opposition to reality. You can then take positive action to save yourself. All you need to forgive is to understand the cycle of pain, and with that understanding necessarily comes connection and compassion.

So, the next time someone wrongs you, you should complain a little bit if that makes you feel better. And, on a certain level you are totally justified in asking: "Why did he do that to me?" It's your right to do so. However, almost always the better question would be: "Why did he do that to himself?" When you hurt someone, you are hurting yourself either through the other person's pain or by cutting yourself off from the connection of your shared humanity with the other. As the external party receiving someone's aggression, you may see yourself as the victim because you are being hurt due to someone else's internal pain, and again, there is a certain level of truth to that. However, you more accurately collateral damage—it is the person himself who is suffering the most internally. In fact, he is hurting so much that he needs to victimize someone else because he thinks that will make himself feel better, when in fact it will only cause regret and/or alienate him further from mankind.

This is all very high minded and esoteric, but it is also so very real. Let me return to my sad little story. Peter broke my heart and wasted my time. He took three years of my life from me in which I devoted nearly all of my free time to him, made life decisions for him, hung on his every word, and endured his endless criticism. Setting aside for now the fact that I am responsible for that because it was my free choice (however insane and inspired by fear), Peter did know how devoted I was to him, and yet he also knew full well that he had no romantic interest in me for most of that time. To the contrary, he was bored and resentful of me, and his resentment fed on his boredom. Why did he do that to me? Sure, fair question. The better one: Why did he do that to himself? Why did he waste three years of his own time with someone for whom he had little feeling?

At this point, we should be satisfied with a general answer because Peter's actions speak for themselves: he obviously was not behaving rationally, not behaving in his own best interests—or mine. Remember, though, I am a hyperlogical person who needs answers, and luckily the specific answer is not difficult to discern. Peter's upbringing and endless string of messy, sexed-up, and destructive relationships are not what builds a person up or makes him feel that he is worthy or capable of a stable, loving relationship. Living that kind of hedonistic lifestyle creates a self-perpetuating cycle: with each sexual escapade, your sexual appetite becomes more difficult to satiate, your self-control weakens, and you harden your heart because you want the sex without the intimacy that naturally flows between human beings in such an act. You do this so many times that soon you can become crippled: you cannot access or recognize your own feelings for another person because you have become too used to shutting off your heart to people, and you never develop the honesty and communication skills that a loving relationship requires to stay alive. This is why Peter found it so difficult to discuss sex or matters of the heart: he was so accustomed to just doing who knows what with God knows whom that the intimacy and trust required to discuss these matters was scary and shameful for him. This must be a very lonely and disconnected existence indeed. Furthermore, there is the distinct possibility that Peter had come to the point at which deep down he felt unworthy or incapable of an adult relationship, and therefore he settled on suffering through what he thought was the next best option—a cold relationship with me. In any event, he also had to live with the fact that he must have known he would eventually hurt me or face a future with me that he didn't want, which either caused him dread or led him to cut me off emotionally, two scenarios that both would have been painful for him.

So, you tell me: Who hurt more? I was deeply and sincerely in love for three years, and though there was a lot of pain as Peter tore at the tatters of my self-esteem and I felt desperation as he lost interest, there was so much joy in opening my heart to him. I gave him my time, my money, and whatever help I could offer, for no other reason than I loved him, and it felt wonderful. As for Peter, those three years were a mix of boredom, foreboding, resentment, confusion, and hopelessness, made worse for the fact that he did not have the warm radiance of true love to balance out or obscure his negative feelings. At least I had that luxury, and though distraught at the breakup, I never doubted my ability to love another. Quite to the contrary, my relationship with Peter was my first significant relationship as a full-fledged adult, beyond any pretense of still being a kid. Given what a phony alpha male I had become, love taught me that I could be a kind and generous person, something I had not realized until that point. Unconditional love is the great affirmation because in our love for the other person, we draw upon our well of generosity and find it to be bottomless. We are humbled by our own depth of goodness. Peter left the relationship having learned little, still too uncomfortable or simply unable to access and give voice to his feelings. He at last accepted his conviction of being unable to handle a monogamous adult relationship. If he was ever happy or grateful about that time, I cannot recall him ever saying so. So, tell me: Who suffered more?

Again, the case with Gary is starker, given the extremity of his personality, experience, and accumulated pain. Indeed, Gary himself articulated at length and I have recorded already that his pain had made him "strong" and taught him many twisted lessons about how to live. He was carrying the pain around with him in the form of memories and axioms that told him to keep other people away, not connect or empathize with them. That is disconnection, which is suffering, and it will breed more suffering.

The specific ways in which this is true are also not difficult to see or imagine. First of all, you can cut off people, and you can cut off emotion. However, you cannot cut off specific emotions. In other words, you can dull your ability to feel: through withdrawal, drugs, sex, or any number of other ways. But, you cannot block sadness, fear, or pain in particular while keeping the good stuff. You cannot pick and choose which emotions you want to feel. Gary did not have an apparent iota of sadness, regret, or remorse at abruptly ending our relationship. As I said in my call to him, this is not the reaction a normal human being has to sadness, but there it is: Gary wasn't sad. He also wasn't happy or in love prior to that, not really, because the universe demands balance. You cannot feel happy at having something but not sad to lose it. You cannot feel love but avoid the loss of love. You certainly don't have to dwell on, suffer from, or internalize the pain of loss, carrying it with you forever, but you cannot escape it either. Again, none of this requires much insight or conjecture on my part, because Gary said it himself: "You can't get too attached to people" or feel too bad about what happens to them. And what is a life without attachment or *connection* with others? That is a life of disconnection, which is pain. This is part of the pain Gary transferred to me in his cycle of pain dynamics.

Gary said he was strong. How strong, though, was he really? Is cutting people off, refusing to cry, eliminating pain from your life, and ignoring the plight of others strength? No. These are defense mechanisms that Gary desperately employed because he was so afraid of the pain he had suffered in his youth. What Gary had erected was emotional armor, and incidentally this kind of armor is quite common, though the degree of trauma in Gary's life had just made his two meters thick. Why wear armor other than the fact that you are afraid? You're afraid of being hurt, of being judged. You are closed, and therefore by definition you must not be open to...what? Life's possibilities, love, true connection with humanity and nature. What is fear but a form of pain? And there it is again: the cycle of pain. Armor is not courage or strength—it is cowardice and fear.

And what is to become of all of this? This also is not too difficult to divine in both general and specific terms. Gary's strength was not strength but hardness formed in order to guard against all of the things he feared. This was the strength of the tree that does not bend. And, as the old saying goes, what happens to the tree that does not bend? It breaks. But, with such a hard tree, it will take quite a tempest to break it, so the inevitable fall will be dramatic. Likewise, the seawall collapses if the wave is strong enough, while the salt marsh absorbs the flow, just as the tree survives by bending.

What could this breaking look like in Gary's place? Well, he was strictly devoted to this vision of a family as his only refuge from a cruel and capricious world. If you cannot allow yourself to truly connect with other people and you forbid yourself from feeling compassion or empathy, how on earth can you have a healthy, loving relationship? How can you raise healthy, happy children nourished by the boundless love of the parents who gave life to them? You can't. You don't need to be a clairvoyant to see that this isn't going to work. And, if the only outlet you currently have for love is your nuclear family, what happens when your parents depart this earth and your sibling becomes absorbed in her own family? Where do you turn for the love of family if you cannot allow yourself to be open to forming new, real, loving connections? You turn to drugs or sex or some other escapist behavior. Or, you settle for a pretend family and slowly burn with the misery and desperation of deeply knowing that it isn't working, that you're playing pretend. The cycle of pain continues and is transmitted to new victims.

So, the cycle of pain makes so much of the world turn, but the irony is that it isn't even real. Pain, it must be acknowledged, cannot be escaped and is usually justified. A parent who loses a child would be made of something unnatural to not feel pain, and who could say that parent didn't have the right to feel that way? However, note that some people go through war and genocide, rape and torture, and yet come out somehow okay in the end. Look at so many of the children of the Holocaust who, a few years after liberation, played the violin, built a new life, and hugged their own children with arms that had numbers burned into them. Then, consider my case: I had a prestigious job, more money than I could spend, no life-threatening health problems, an intact family, and the opportunity to travel to some of the most exciting and beautiful places on earth. I had been educated in the best schools, had met more world leaders in a year than most people will in their life, and had been encouraged from a young age to pursue my dreams. I had led a charmed life. And yet, I was the one who was so depressed that I wanted to kill myself. Does that make any sense?

No, because pain is not real. It is in your mind. You can't touch it, smell it, taste it, hear it, or see it. Pain shows you are human, and is natural. As doctors will tell you that physical pain is your body's way of telling you something is wrong. Emotional pain tells you that you are not okay with something, and that is typically perfectly understandable or justified. Sustained, prolonged, pain, however, is suffering, which means you are still fighting with the reality of the situation. Sure, even years after the fact when some smell or sound or situation reminds you of someone you lost, it is natural that pain will well up from the hole that person's departure left in you. Ceaselessly carrying around the pain, however, means you are holding on to it and creating it for yourself. Of course this is not a conscious decision, unless you are a masochist. It is subconscious because whatever you have lost is seen by your ego as an affront to its being. If in your own mind you were the loving and protective husband and are now without a wife, then you are no longer yourself. Your life has lost value. But is that true? Is it real?

The reality is that any moment holds an infinite number of possibilities regardless of what happened to you a moment, a day, a week, a month, a year, or a lifetime before. And, because everyone's suffering is ultimately in their own minds as a hell they make for themselves, it cannot be compared or contrasted between individuals. One person suffers the horrors of war and flourishes, whereas the other commits suicide after losing face at work. Can we say the first person's suffering was worse than the second person's? No, because the suffering is a result of whatever thoughts or subconscious rantings are going on in each person's mind, and we have no way of knowing those. This is also the hope of pain. At any moment, if examined and seen in the light of day, the fallacy of pain becomes impossible to miss. We may tell ourselves that we are worthless because it seems nobody loves us, but life's possibilities are still endless, and we have the ability at any moment to drop that thought and focus our attention on something else. And this is why there is no shame in pain: we all have the ability to create the most elaborate cages out of almost nothing, and we all have the ability to pick the locks and free ourselves. All we need is for once to know what we are doing, to bring the pain to a conscious level.

So much of human behavior is driven by the ceaseless cycle of pain, which is powered by thoughts that have little basis in reality. This fact creates endless depressing ironies. The beauty of life and the power of humanity, however, is that at any moment we can decide to be pain sinks. We can end the cycle of pain just through nonreaction or even better, compassion to other people's pain. This is very doable if we just understand bad behavior as the expression of pain, and it is a simple commitment we can all make.

As for ourselves, if we examine and question our pain, we can put it in its proper place as a memory that is occasionally awakened by reality. When we do this, we no longer pollute our environment with our pain and drive others to react to it with negative thoughts or emotions. Maybe this isn't heaven on earth, but it is far from our own private hells in which we spend far too much time.

In my own case, this was all something that took a very long time to understand. I first unconsciously stumbled on all of this years ago without realizing the wisdom of what I uncovered. When I first moved away to China after my undergraduate studies, suddenly my whole family started having lots of problems with one another. There were arguments and physical altercations, people moved away, were cut off, and stopped speaking. None of it had anything to do with me and was all a result of long-festering problems between them, and the different sides were pitted against one another as everyone's grievances became intertwined. Oddly enough, some of them tried to involve me in all of it and even stopped speaking to me for years, long after they had made up with each other. All the while I was not even involved. At that time, I realized that the extreme pain that had built up over so many years needed to be released, and I was just one distant outlet for it. I saw how sad they all were and how happy I was at that time, even though I was always the outsider in the family. That was it, however. It was *because* I was the outsider and not mixed up in all of their pain that I was happy. From that moment, I understood that whatever they did to me when I was younger, it hurt them much more than it hurt me. I got over it, but they were still suffering. It was the best they could do. They did their best with what they had to be good parents and siblings, and in the end I was nobody's victim—I was more fortunate than the lot of them. I forgave everything.

Unfortunately, the logic did not extend in a broader sense to other relationships or experiences. After the hell of the five years of my life from 2008 to 2013, however, I was able to put all of the pieces together from the books and apply these lessons and paradigms to what had just happened to me. Gary, however, was not able to do that. That poor child had been uprooted from his home and made to live in penury; moved away from his parents; and was threatened, isolated, raped, and tormented. He was so afraid of being hurt that he shut off and crippled his own ability to empathize or form a meaningful relationship with anyone outside his nuclear family. He objectified all people as serving some purpose for him, and easily discarded them when he moved on. To the extent he worshipped his family, he objectified them as idols on pedestals without equal in the evil world. For him, a healthy respect for family values had turned into an idolization set up in opposition to the cruel and dangerous world. This was all his armor, underneath which was just the little boy snatched from his bed in the middle of the night who didn't want to be hurt again. This is a tragedy.

I remember one time I wanted to give Gary a pleasant little surprise, so without calling ahead I knocked on his door one night. In my hand was a small gift. Gary was almost beside himself. He was nervous, and even after he let me in was totally on edge. The situation was tense for me also, and he gave me a stern talking-to, explaining how frightened he was and how I was never to do that again: this all in what is often considered to be the safest city on earth. It was all a result of the incident five years earlier when his stalker-cum-host would follow his every move by accessing his computer and mobile phone, calling him nonstop all day using multiple phone numbers, and assume identities. Can you imagine living in such fear? That is what a mind-made hell looks like.

Do you hate someone like this? *Can* you hate someone like this? All you can do once you understand the crushing reality of Gary's accumulated pain is empathize with him. It's not his fault, and he didn't deserve any of this. After what life had done to him, he did the best he could. Consider the fact that he spoke his feelings to me as abruptly as he felt them. He never lied to me. He did not cut off contact with me initially or tell me to leave him alone when he dumped me. In fact, it was me who repeatedly contacted him with my sadness and confusion in order to get some reaction from him to validate myself. All he wanted was not to feel guilt or more pain. If I could accuse him of something, what would it even be other than that he could have been a bit more sensitive in his delivery? He did the best he could in the way he knew how to live his life, and I cannot begrudge him for that. I can't even say I forgive him completely, because this implies some sort of effort or decision-making process. I am forgiveness for him. It is my breath.

Because I didn't know then what I know now, I was a conductor for pain rather than a sink. I took all of the pain and painful lessons that caused him to feel and do as he did, and I internalized those. I allowed these to fester into a deep depression, and I attempted to bring him down into the depths with me. I tried to hurt myself, and I made the people who cared about me sad and worried. I polluted the world with my pain, and I did not acknowledge or empathize with his. The beauty, for which I am so thankful, is that I have since acquired the insight to do this—to feel other people's pain and react with compassion and empathy: making forgiveness automatic. Of course I had this ability, as do all people, but it is a learned skill that requires practice, as does gratitude. Once you practice enough, it becomes something like second nature, and that's where I am now. I often need to remind myself, but soon I realize again that forgiveness is always there.

Would I like him in my life or take back my cutting off of relations? No, I would not. I do not want that kind of sickness in my life, and given the state of Gary's pain and ego, there is little that I can do to help him. He must save himself. One day he will be touched by love or tragedy or something else to wake him up. It's his journey. What I would do differently is to remove the negativity and reactivity and drama that I added to the situation and therefore add no further momentum to the cycle of pain. Now that I live in forgiveness, however, I have forgiven him for his harshness and myself for my foolishness. I can move on with my life, dream again, and love again. I am free, which indeed is the greatest gift I can give myself.

Chapter 13: The transformative power of suffering

Sometimes I feel sorry for myself, though not in the way I used to. I do not wallow in self-pity, as was so evident in the first part of this book. Instead, I see my past self as another person, and I think about what he went through, and I know he didn't deserve it. I want to help him so he doesn't have to go through all of that suffering. I want him to come out with the wisdom and strength he emerged with in the end but without having to feel so much pain in the process. Then again, however, who is the original sinner who deserves the suffering that he feels? Nobody. None of us deserves to be hurt, and yet we all suffer to varying degrees in our lives. Why?

The truth is that the wisdom and strength we need to navigate this world are often imparted through experience. Using Ram Dass' explanation for spiritual growth, how many people actually evolve solely by reading some compelling books or having a particularly effective teacher? I have yet to meet or hear of such a person. Perhaps this can occur in monastic communities or similar environments, where the monks live, sleep, eat, and breathe the teachings from a young age, as does every other person with whom they are in close contact. However, most people need an opening, something that readies them to receive wisdom and strength.

I gather that if you haven't thrown this book down in frustration and confusion at the self-absorbed, self-pitying writer, then you have probably in your own way become ready.

At the risk of being didactic, the question must first be asked: What is wisdom, and what is strength? This is important because we need both. Wisdom is not knowledge. It is not facts and figures. Wisdom is the ability to think and act using knowledge, understanding, and insight: something akin to judgment. So, we take knowledge, and then we contemplate and deliberate in order to gain insight and understanding. Theoretically, this should be enough to yield wisdom, but the missing link is experience. Experience is what provides the subject matter of our lives, and it's what helps us by providing food for contemplation. On a certain level, we are the center of our own experience, and hence experience can endow us with the passion to devote our mind energy to serious deliberation. What sort of experience, however, could arouse the type of passion needed to wake our mind up out of its typical pattern of repetitive and useless thinking in order to undertake purposeful thinking? Anything out of the ordinary enough to wake us up out of the muck for a moment should do just fine, but upon reflection, how often does extreme joy or pleasure or delight drive us to think? These are simple feelings that do not inspire us to exercise our minds because they are fine just as they are.

However, the opposite end of the spectrum—pain, confusion, betrayal, or other such negative experiences—do not sit well with us. The vengeful self wants to know who to blame for them, whereas the more constructive self wants to see what it can learn from them, how to avoid them in the in the future, or how to harness them and transmute them into positivity.

And, what does negativity cause for us? Pain. Pain, however, is merely a sensation; whereas suffering is pain carried forward even after the initial irritant is gone. Suffering is pain stretched out over time, and we need time to contemplate. In this way, suffering and our desire to avoid it are often what drive the growth and change that bring us to wisdom. When we are wise, we think and behave differently than when we were ignorant, foolish, immature or *inexperienced*. We change.

What about strength? If armor is weakness and cowardice in the face of fear, strength must be the opposite: courage in the face of fear. And, what is the opposite of wearing armor? It is vulnerability: it is not wearing armor. Vulnerability is the willingness to pursue a path knowing that you will face whatever slings and arrows life will throw your way, both known and unknown, and still remain who you are—no defense mechanisms. You know it's going to hurt at some point, but you do it anyway because it's that important to you: you care enough, love enough, feel enough to take the risk.

As we take that walk, facing the trials and tribulations in order to get where we think we want to be, we will undoubtedly suffer at some point. One of the clearest examples again is Jesus Christ, whose passion, as epitomized by his trip through Jerusalem and torment on the cross, was necessary for the resurrection and salvation of mankind. The funny thing though is that once we arrive, we usually find the place is not exactly what we had hoped, or perhaps it is but not for long, or maybe our indefatigable human imagination conjures up something better. Indeed, many Christians await the Second Coming, as our bleeding earth remains so far from heaven. So, after some time at our destination we find it either never was or cannot remain the Promised Land because all life is change. We usually realize this through some form of suffering, and then our wisdom tells us it is time to move on, and our strength gives us the courage to move on despite being vulnerable. Of course, we can always put on our armor, but then we get no hints on where to go because we numb the pain and suffering that is there to guide us.

Putting it all together, thriving in the journey of life that is never-ending change also requires us to grow and change. Growth and change require wisdom and strength, and the most effective (or perhaps only) way to acquire these things is by experiencing suffering. However, we can suffer consciously only when we allow ourselves the courage to be vulnerable. Otherwise, we wear the armor and do not hurt nearly as much, but we also are not aware of what life is trying to tell us. We become static as the world passes us by until, if we are lucky, our armor cracks and falls off, broken open by suffering. Either way, when we have suffered enough, we are able to cast aside our old notions that led us to suffer in the first place. We change.

Life is a road with many forks. We always take the wrong one, again and again, until we can no longer bear our suffering. When we finally reach that point, we change or we die. When we wear our armor of certainty—the certainty of who we think we are or how life should be according to the story we tell ourselves in order to remain static—we move slowly and make the wrong decisions or stay where we are. So, suffering is the goad that drives us in the right direction. It's what finally tells us to go left when our inner demon, our ego, keeps telling us to go right. That is the role of suffering.

I have driven some of my friends crazy with this. They come to me for advice on relationships, jobs, and some important decision. Although they are different people laboring over very different situations, I never cease to be amazed by how often they persist in making the wrong choices again and again and again, as I once did. My response to their dismay is always the same: "You just haven't suffered enough. When you've suffered so much that you can't take it anymore, you will change. You will have no choice then."

These dynamics are obvious in my own story. I wore my alpha-male armor to protect myself and shut out an unknowable number of people, experiences, and lessons. As my alienation and disconnection became more profound, I fell deeper into my own story of just needed that one special relationship to give my life meaning. I just needed one person to love, who in turn would love and protect me from the cruel world, lifting me out of my loneliness. As my life became smaller and smaller, I became more convinced of this egoic narrative and even more intent on seeing it fulfilled. I shut out and cut myself off from more and more, all the while missing the obvious signs that it wasn't working. I just kept going deeper and deeper until the fallacy of my story and of my pain was revealed. When the story unraveled, and I had suffered so intensely, only then was I finally able to change. I couldn't bear the pain any longer, so I was faced with the choice: change or die. I chose change. I chose life.

When he left the stage of my life, Gary was committed as ever to wearing his armor, following the same path. His family aside, he was all alone in the terrible world, completely disconnected by his own choice. Remember, connection is what allows us to share joy and love and compassion for others. However, through connection we are also open to others' pain and suffering, which we take on through empathy. Connection also makes us aware of and responsible for how our actions impact other people. Pain, suffering, responsibility: these are things Gary feared and vocally rejected, so he shut off connection with other people to spare himself.

The sad thing is that Gary's story, his ego, was far too clever in its foundational myth. It invented a nearly fail-proof mechanism for self-preservation. Suffering is what wakes us up and points us to the right direction. Gary worked hard to avoid it, but of course his life, like everyone else's, involved pain, loss, and misfortune. Convinced, however, of the cruel nature of the world and committed to an existence of disconnection, Gary interpreted any suffering as further proof of the veracity of his story. The world is terrible and will hurt you, so put on some more armor and withdraw further from it. Seek refuge in family. This leads us to where we were some time ago: What happens when the family passes on, and what happens when the new family he aims to create inevitably fails to live up to his unrealistic expectations of being his salvation? He will be trying to force real people to fit his ideal and absolutist vision, hardly a recipe for success. At what point will he change or die, or will he just continue to sink slowly into despair? This wasting process will of course be aided by the inevitable aging of his body and fading of his good looks which, in his own self-declared vanity, occupy so much of his attention. In Gary's case, suffering will only strengthen his ego unless and until it destroys that ego.

Suffering batters us until we break open just a little and allow ourselves to receive wisdom and emerge stronger, and then we suffer more and grow more thereafter. It seems like a Sisyphean journey, but with each round of suffering we emerge better prepared to deal with what comes our way if we are open to taking the alternate path. The alternative is to hunker down and close ourselves. We might not hurt as much because we put on our armor and are less vulnerable to all of the external threats in the world. However, we also close ourselves to joy, connection, love, and all of the positive things that require us to show and share ourselves. It's a classic case of risk and reward. Those who take the risk really live, and life is full of ups and downs, and in fact life requires downs if it is to have ups. A mountain with no valleys is just a plateau. A life of caution and fear *may* insulate one from some of the undulations that can bring it high and bring it low, but that is the way of stagnation and disconnection. The choice is yours. In the end, it may not be a choice at all, because the armor inevitably cracks, the seawall crumbles, and the tree that doesn't bend breaks.

Creating our own suffering

The world will throw enough challenges and pain in peoples' ways to occupy a lifetime, but yet we cannot help but complicate things further by creating our own obstacles. The most common way we do this is to think ourselves into a bad situation. For human beings, thought and perception are our own private reality. All of our preconceived notions, prejudices, philosophies, interpretations, judgments, suspicions, and so on are shaped by our experience, and we in turn view the world through their prisms. A hotel doorman holds open the door. A Hollywood star so accustomed to this may not even notice, so it does not even enter his or her reality, or perhaps it leads to annoyance if the doorman did not act with adequate speed or courtesy. You or I might feel that nice, pampered feeling, like we're pretending to be someone important for a moment. A vagabond might feel grateful just to be let in the door. One event, but three different realities, three different perceptions, three different emotional reactions. One person's heaven can be another's hell.

This is not a new philosophy. All sorts of writers over millennia have commented on the power of thought:

- Buddha (5-6th Century BCE): "All that we are is the result of what we have thought. The mind is everything. What we think, we become."

- Shakespeare (around 1600): "There is nothing either good or bad but thinking makes it so."

- Maya Angelou (1993): "What you're supposed to do when you don't like a thing is change it. If you can't change it, change the way you think about it."

Because thinking is what shapes peoples' perceptions of reality, the world, and their lives, it is shocking how often it is overlooked, how much thinking goes on by itself below consciousness. This was the first major realization I had once I started to recover from my near suicide—how there was a voice in my head that dictated how I perceived and reacted to everything. Not surprisingly, thanks to Eckhart Tolle, once I became aware of this voice who was not me, I realized how sad, angry, and hurt it was—I was deeply depressed after all!

Once again I was fortunate in a sense for the extremity of my situation. Being so severely depressed contemporaneously while learning about thinking, the ego, presence, and so on made these concepts come to life so clearly for me. Once I read about thinking and what it could do, the thoughts screaming at me suddenly became so clear. There was no process of comprehending what the authors were saying. I could hear it in my head! There were all of these thoughts, and I was not thinking them—they were thinking me! What they said made me suffer so.

This, however, raises a critical distinction between types of suffering. Conscious suffering is mostly what is described in the previous chapter. It is feeling pain due to the circumstances of your life, which you pass through with your eyes wide open. There is no way to absolutely avoid it, though you may don your armor to protect yourself, to the detriment of your own ability to grow, change, and flourish.

The type of suffering I was undergoing was largely unconscious. It was driven by thoughts that were repetitive, compulsive, pointless, *unconscious*, and totally unnecessary. Whatever was happening to and around me might have been wonderful—and indeed much of it was—but my unconscious thinking directed me to ignore, suspect, reject, or otherwise twist it. I felt pain not necessarily because of anything that happened but simply as a result of how my mind was putting things together. Sure, difficult situations arose, but remember—pain is not real. The poor village child whose whole family is killed in an ethnic genocide turns out just fine in the end, whereas the rich kid who didn't get a new car for his birthday overdoses on drugs. Feeling pain is certainly justified, especially in light of our accumulated experiences that drive how we perceive events, but how far we carry that pain depends on our state of mind.

Depression makes pain dynamics so crystal clear because it is the monstrous extreme of the processes of pain at work. As I write this, I have just listened to commentary about the depression of beloved comic Robin Williams, who recently committed suicide. Although some of the commentators have clearly never themselves been or intimately known someone depressed, some hit the nail right on the head. I believe it was Larry King who described depression as a black hole. It sucks up and feeds on everything. A depressed person could hear that he won the lottery, and his reaction would be the same as if you told him he lost his job. Everything is bad. Everything is just more proof of whatever the internal narrative is that is making life so unbearable. If you have not experienced it, you cannot truly understand it because it is insanity to the nth degree.

I cringe to think about how little empathy I had for depressed people prior to my own descent into the abyss. I would always ask, "What are they so upset about? What's the big deal? Why don't they just get over it? People have bigger problems than they do!" What I didn't understand is that maybe there is no big deal, or maybe there is—it doesn't matter. Depression is a mental illness, and it's a hell we make for ourselves. Of course, you would be sad in the face of bad events and happy in the face of good events, but depression is sadness no matter what because your mind is telling you something terrible, no matter what. Suicide is the logical conclusion of this state of being because there is no reason to live if everything is always bad, all the time. People who commit or try to commit suicide don't want to die. They just want to make the pain go away.

"Suicide is the most selfish act" or some similar variation is a very common saying. This is, in a way, completely correct, but not in the way it was intended. Depression and suicide are completely "selfish" because a person cannot think beyond himself or herself. Everything that happens is twisted by one's mind to be some negative commentary on one's life, oneself, the world's treatment of one, one's place in the world—and so on. One is the center of one's own universe. A depressed person is completely trapped in the story his or mind has made up—his or her ego. It is the height of self-obsession, the most pure state of disconnectedness, of isolation. In other words, it is the most advanced stage of a negative ego, because everything refers to and reflects upon the ego. It's all about you, and you are all alone.

Depression, disconnectedness, suicide: if these are the last things we want from our lives, then what do we really want? Let us once again find the truth in identifying opposites. Depression is complete disconnectedness, believing totally in the story being told by the mind, which happens to be a sad story. What then is the opposite of this situation? It is connectedness, complete unity with life, and not believing the story. We can lazily refer to this as "happiness," but it is more than that—it is joy. This distinction is critical, not a fastidious point. Happy and sad are point-in-time reactions. Something unpleasant occurs, so you get sad, whereas something pleasant makes you happy. In the removal of the stimuli, you return to a neutral state. This is perfectly logical. Joy, like depression, is a state of being. They are not quite opposites because depression is caused by a mental illness that corrupts everything. Its opposite is something like euphoria, which is typically drug-induced. It is happiness no matter what, another (very rare) type of insanity.

Joy is something like the opposite of depression, so it is total connectedness, complete unity with life regardless of what the story says. What does that look like? If it is unconscious thinking that makes us constantly disconnected, the absence of such thought, or not listening to or believing such thought, drives connectedness and unity. How so? As previously discussed, all of this thinking is driven by and feeds into a character called the ego, which is all of your accumulated experiences, thoughts, and emotions. The ego provides a barrier between us and life because we can experience our life and everything that comes into it only through the prism of the ego. We stand on top of the building to get a clear view of the whole city, but we don't really see the city. If we're an optimist or a proud local, what we see instead is that amazing place full of life, with things happening, progress being

101

made, quick and creative. If we're from out of town or not a city person, we see a harsh existence where people are rushing around, just cogs in an uncaring, polluted, and impersonal machine, struggling just to get by. Both interpretations create a veil between us and life—either by ignoring or fixating on the unpleasant aspects of the city. We never really know the city.

Of course, the veil over our eyes is created by the doings of our unconscious mind, our ego, and everyone's is unique. Because each ego is different and can see things only through one prism, we cannot fully relate to anyone or anything else. We are alone, and we are stuck in our own little world, together with our ego. The world may change, but as long as our ego does not, we fundamentally stay the same. We just get older, change jobs, get hurt, make more or less money, and so forth. Of course, as we hunker down, we do feel some pain and are perhaps jolted by some dramatic experiences. If our pain does not bring us closer to reality—meaning we do not gain wisdom or strength, or if we never become aware of the ego—then the ego will typically either become stronger or adapt to fit the circumstances. The unconscious suffering continues. This is a static life, because life is constant change, including ourselves. The ego tries to make us stay the same and will do so even when all else fails, when all our attempts to hold on to things come up short.

In the absence of unconscious thought or when we ignore or don't believe the thinking, nothing separates us from the world. This is what *being present*, the most popular of New Age buzzwords, means. We just are. We see. We smell. We hear. We taste. We actually don't add anything to the world as we experience it. We are satisfied. We connect with whatever is around us because there is nothing in the way, and there is no other alternative reality. In this sense, we can never really be alone. This state is necessary if we are to be joyful. If depression and the ego are static, joy is motion. The world changes, so our experience changes. We change. Life is change, and joy means we are keeping up with life, not fighting it, not trying to keep it in conformation with our view of how it should be.

Sure, at times we may want to change something, and we should do that if it is in our power. The power to change things is part of reality itself. However, rejecting and not surrendering to reality, this is how we become disconnected and static.

If we are keeping up with the world and experiencing it as it is, there is our place. We don't need to try and change ourselves in order to receive life. We know we will change as needed, automatically. This is called *worthiness*. We are worthy of life because we are there. Our humanity means we are alive, experiencing everything, and we are not disconnected by creating our own inner thought-world—we are part of it all. We are worthy. Joy comes from an inherent sense of worthiness. We are enough. To live life joyfully is our birthright. And, embedded in this is equality, because everyone else has the same right, by virtue of their humanity. We are all in this together. Equality and connectedness therefore imply one another. So does empathy, because if we are equal and connected, how can we not open our hearts, understand one another, and feel with each other when we are open to doing so? This is all unity. In fact, it is so much so that I am sure this passage bears reading and rereading, because the concepts become difficult to separate—at least this is how I still feel reading spiritual and religious books. It all starts to melt together.

This process of joining with the larger unity, of finally ceasing to bring suffering upon myself by no longer throwing up barriers to the world and people around me, happened slowly. And then—once I understood—very quickly. My suffering and disconnection grew over those five years in Singapore and eventually bore down on me as the crushing weight of depression. I could not escape my own mind. After the attempt at suicide, I realized that the story must have been false because nothing I told myself I needed had come to pass, and there I still was. That I walked out of that pharmacy empty handed opened up infinite possibilities, but I was in no physical or emotional shape to seize them.

The recurring thought patterns, particularly the movie in my mind of being abandoned, of having wasted some of my best years, kept playing over and over again on a loop. In psychology this is called *rumination*. Using what is called *cognitive therapy*, my therapist began to free me of this. In layman's terms, the basic assumption is that negative emotions are driven by an underlying negative thought, and the therapy seeks to identify and combat those thoughts. When you realize and then give voice to the fact that you feel hopeless because you think "No one will ever love me," you realize how crazy that sounds. Six billion people in the world, and no one will ever love you? Why, because you had two or three people toss you aside? Simply shining a light on these assumptions and becoming aware of them is a critical first step and points to still more underlying thoughts. Why were you dumped—maybe because you were not worthy? My repetitive, compulsive thoughts had become so strong that I could not escape them, and I needed drugs—antidepressants, antianxiety medications, and sleeping pills—just to give myself space to undertake these thought exercises. Without the drugs, I am not sure if I would have been able to gather up even the mental energy, motivation, or courage to begin exploring and questioning my thoughts.

As the depression lifted and the yoke of my depressive mind slowly slipped off, I became suspended in a psychological limbo. I had already worked through the logic of how my life had arrived at that point and the motivations and reasons for Peter, Gary, myself and all the others for doing what they had done: becoming what they had become. With so many of the thoughts gone, my mind didn't know what to think. With so many of the questions settled, my mind didn't have any food. The books told me not to think anything, but I still did not feel joyful. I was no longer hopeless, but neither was I hopeful. I knew that each time I arose from my bed offered me the opportunity to go and seize the innumerable promises of the day, but I didn't know where to go or what to do.

This was my state when I went on my trip to New Zealand, which jolted me with an explosion of sensory experience: the million hues of green in the forests' racket of flora, the fierceness of the cold rain as we scaled the mountain, the pounding of the waves thrashing the shore as the storms raged, the exhaustion at having climbed above the snowline, the noble silence and enormity of the mountains piercing the sky. New Zealand reminded me I was alive and showed me where I could go—anywhere. It had always been one of my dreams to do an adventure trip there, and I did it, my foot mangled as it was. As I said earlier, it put me back on my feet, but how? It smacked me in the face with extremes of reality so intense that they called for no interpretation or labeling. For the first time ever I was experiencing a state of no thinking, while not feeling as if I was missing out. In fact, when the old narratives came back and seized my attention—which they still do to this day and probably always will from time-to-time—it was an annoyance. I caught myself following the dead-end, depressive, angry thoughts only so far before I was able to wake up and avoid developing a full-blown emotional response.

When I came back to Singapore, I was lucky that my project would end just a few weeks later, giving me some time on the beach—without staffing. The last few weeks of the project also brought me to Hong Kong, allowing me to put one foot firmly in the future and away from the setting of my sad story. I then had months without real work, due to my surgery and recovery, training in Dubai, and a trip back to New York. Then, when I arrived in Hong Kong, I was immediately sent off to briefly stand in for someone on a project in San Francisco, a place I had never been. This allowed me do some more exploring in a very low-stress environment. It was a week of hard work, but given that I was just a substitute for another team member, the stakes were low for my career. Finally, right after that, in Virginia I took a few weeks to train my company's new hires from around the world, a fun, relaxing, and very rewarding experience.

This three-month-or-so period gave me more time to read, and I devoured the books on my reading list with a ferocious appetite. Without the sad story always in my mind, I turned over all of the concepts of the books and began to see their truths in my life. Without my ego separating me from everyone, I dropped so much of the negativity and aggression that I had toward people that I never even realized was there. I laid the alpha male to rest. I made a conscious decision to avoid the people who had neglected or cast me aside through my moves and troubles and illnesses, spending my time with the few people who cared. I was surrounded by love. I loved back. I filled my life with positivity, and although I had a little breakdown once every week or two, in general I felt a near-constant gratitude, which felt exactly as all of the books described it.

Before leaving Singapore, I knew the real test would be meeting face-to-face with Peter and Gary, the two people who had caused me so much pain. Peter visited me in the hospital when I was recovering from surgery. I told him I forgave him, to which he responded that he had never done anything wrong to me. I explained calmly about how he had made me feel those years when he constantly criticized me and how his failure to own up to his true feelings (or lack thereof) for me wasted at least two years of my life—though I also took responsibility for staying with and even clinging more tightly to him when it was clear he wasn't interested anymore. What he said to me then opened my heart with empathy and again brought to life so much I had read. First, he recounted how being with me had interrupted so much of his fun, hedonistic, and destructive lifestyle, but he did not hold that against me. Then, he claimed to have no knowledge that I was even coming back from France, even though that was always the plan, and I had told him I didn't have a choice. I had made a commitment to my company to return to Singapore after my six-month transfer to the Paris office. Finally, he made the following statement: "I don't know why you can't get over it. We were only together for *two* years."

I am not rehashing a litany of complaints against him here, but this really did cause compassion to bloom in my heart. Why did he do that to me? That had been my mind-set. Now the more relevant question became obvious: Why did he do that to himself? He knew he was bored out of his mind and resentful of me but stayed with me anyway. He was so eager to get rid of me that he didn't even bother to pay any attention to the terms of my transfer to Paris, this while we were supposed to be starting a life together. It was all so unimportant or so unbearable for him—interrupting all his fun—that he did not even recall that it had been *three* years—not two—that we had been together. Why did he do that to himself? Knowing his whole story as well as I did, I realized he did not even value his own time enough to distinguish two from three years. He couldn't imagine anything better for himself than to settle. He was that hopeless, that desperate. A year or two or three of his life meant little to him because his ego prevented him from imagining something different and better.

I was overcome with emotion, and Peter thought he had said something to upset me. He hugged me, said he felt bad for disturbing me—at this point the blood was pouring out of my nose—and left. I knew I would never see him again. What I knew that he never will is that I cried for him. I was overwhelmed with compassion and empathy. I saw what he had done to himself, and I even understood the hidden dynamics driving it all. I already knew full well what I had done to myself, and I felt a connection to him that I never had before. We had both been so wounded together and didn't even know it. The difference was that I was waking up with the insight I was getting, while he was by his own account returning to his recent life and behaviors, falling back further into the dream of his life story, his ego. I saw myself having done that so many times, gone down the same wrong path, again and again. I felt so lucky at that moment. I didn't know why then, but I realized that later I was thankful that my pain had finally goaded me in the right direction.

The nonmeeting with Gary was totally different but produced the same result. I contacted him telling him that I was free during my recovery period and wanted to see him one last time before I left for good. He responded with a few angry and impatient texts, and I let him go. We didn't even meet, but I saw that things with him were still the same, and because of his extreme life story filled with so much suffering, I still wonder if he will ever wake up before he destroys himself.

He was angry and could not forgive me, but why? After all, his ex-boyfriend, the one with whom he had broken up right before he reconnected with me, had done something soap opera dramatic, vengeful, and terrible to him—more than once! And yet, when Gary and I first began our relationship, on several occasions he tried to mend fences with the guy. I wondered why and asked him. Gary said something to effect of that the two shared so many good times that it was a shame to be on bad terms. At the time, I took this for forgiveness, and it was one of the things that led me to believe early on that Gary's pain had made him a more understanding person. I, on the other hand, had done no such thing to him. I collapsed. I nearly died for grief after losing him, the combined suffering of those years finally overwhelming me. I never did anything to him other than remaining in contact with his lesbian friends—whom I mistook for my friends— and I did not bad-mouth him to them but rather sought to understand the situation and have some company at that time when I was alone. Indeed, the only rebuke or challenge I ever made to him was when I spoke to him on the phone after returning from Thanksgiving break. At that time, I asked him how he could react so coldly and told him he could have tried to do things in a more sensitive way.

So what was the difference here? How could he "forgive" the one who had gone to such dramatic lengths to hurt him and hate the one who had hurt so much? Only one answer seemed to make sense. His ex was angry, aggressive, and cruel toward him. Those were things that Gary had understood and experienced. He was used to that because he had experienced so much of it. Indeed, given some of the stories he told me during those disturbing talks when I had first began to fear for our relationship, he himself had also perpetrated a lot of anger, aggression, and cruelty on other people. When I expressed shock at Gary's stories, he seemed almost pleased with or proud of his behavior. As I explained previously, during these times I always made excuses for him. Aggression, hate, anger, taking advantage of someone: these were things he knew and could relate to, a normal part of his world, as he had explained so clearly. That explains his nonchalant reaction to his former boyfriend's behavior. Remember, never once did he use words relating to forgiveness or compassion—he just wanted to still have contact with the guy or make their inevitable social interactions less awkward.

As for me, in his books what was my unforgivable crime? Very simple: I made him feel. That last time he visited me, he cracked for just a moment. "No you won't be [alright]." The trembling lip. I made him feel guilty and responsible for what he had done, leading me down a path of marriage and children and moving overseas before abruptly and without warning dumping me. For just a second, he felt my pain along with me. Here were empathy and compassion. But remember, these require connection. These necessitate the feeling of bad feelings. This is why I was unforgivable. Gary had been through so much pain and was so frightened that he made his whole life about disconnection. He did not want to feel those feelings anymore. He was "amoral" and reveled in not caring about the impact of his actions on other people because that's what life had taught him, and he could no longer bear the sadness. His ego had become so advanced, his story so elaborate, as to make a virtue of isolation. It is a celebration of fear and a rejection of our shared humanity. I reminded him of that humanity, and for that he never spoke to me again—to do so would have been too dangerous to his egoic worldview.

And yet, he deserved none of it. That little boy, plucked out of his bed in the middle of the night to be brought to a foreign land, was totally innocent. As he grew, he put on more armor to protect himself, which was the only way he knew to react. Now, understanding my own journey, I recognized anew what kind suffering he must have felt and how difficult it would be to banish his ego's grip on him. He had such a weight of accumulated pain, and his ego's logic caused even more pain to reinforce its own story. For the first time, I did not feel sorry for him. I did not feel pity or sympathy. I felt empathy. I felt compassion. I could relate to his sad and dramatic and unstable life because the dynamics of pain, fear, and isolation were the same as mine and everyone else's. It was the humanity we shared, and none of us deserved any of what we had been through. No one ever does. As with my recent experience with Peter, I think it was in that moment that I first truly connected with Gary and understood him. At this point, forgiveness was not an option—it became a state of being.

These meetings did not signify only a critical break with the past, a letting go of baggage, so the cliché goes. They also represented a first step beyond *understanding* the concepts of true empathy, compassion, and forgiveness to *feeling* and *living* them. I had already found a degree of peace in the slowing down off my incessant unconscious thought processes, improving of my ability to ignore, or just observing my inner monologue and the slackening of my highly developed ego's grip on my mind. The difference was that now my inner peace had created a space that allowed the outer dynamics of connected living to take hold. Beyond not harassing myself with ego-driven self-criticism and pity, I found more patience and understanding for other people and external situations. Beyond my intellectual understanding of Peter's and Gary's behavior and my sympathy for their situations, I could actively relate to them with compassion and empathy.

Forgiveness worked the opposite way. There is a saying with many variations that forgiveness begins with oneself. In my case, I was harder on myself than on others, and once I was able to be forgiveness for Gary and Peter by understanding their suffering and the reasons behind it, I was able to forgive myself. I had put myself into those situations because I was suffering, and I stuck with them despite the suffering it had caused me—in part because I gave both Gary and Peter the benefit of the doubt. I had been *generous* and *kind* in my thinking, two adjectives I rarely associated with my alpha-male persona. I caused myself a lot of pain and took responsibility for that, and I did not blame Gary and Peter for what they had done, however callous or insensitive, because they had done far worse to themselves than they had done to me. All of us, if we had known better, would have done better.

And such was the virtuous cycle that firmly took root in my life. Awareness led to peace that encouraged connection that engendered compassion that made an opening for empathy that gave rise to forgiveness, and so on. All of the good stuff reinforced other good stuff, and soon these concepts lost their integrity—the many pieces became one. The process of awakening and rebirth gathered an unstoppable and irreversible momentum. This process will never be finished as long as I live, and there will be many reversals and setbacks, but no more so than as rocks and trees and other debris can divert the flow of a river. The river never stands still, there can be all sorts of externally caused disturbances, and it can even double over on itself, but it always flows toward the sea.

Chapter 14: Isolation and connection
- the Law of Reciprocity

My pursuits of Jonah, Peter, and Gary had all unfolded according to the same logic. The circumstances had been the same but for their rising severity. I was at a low point in my life and needed someone to make me feel good about myself: wanted, less lonely, and more important. As I began to feel increasingly helpless, I felt that I needed someone to protect me. As people often say, these were my needs in the relationship.

This has become so commonplace in the vernacular that I don't think anyone really asks the question: Is that true? Did I really need someone to protect me? Did I need to feel more special? What would happen to me and who would I be without those things? The answer became clear after my attempt at suicide—nothing. Nothing happened. I still lived, the world still turned, and every day might just have been the best day of my life. What became so clear is that these needs are just thoughts—conditions of the egoic narrative, which is not real. And, what is one of the most unfortunate effects the ego has on us? The ego isolates us. It puts a veil between the world as it is and our perception, which becomes warped by the ego's logic.

What does this look like in terms of human relationships? When we need something, we look for someone to supply it. That person becomes our supplier, our dealer. He is a means to an end. We are self-centeredly using him to serve our ego's needs. For me, Peter was my hero, my savior. However, to his colleague he was someone who helped with the work. To the guy at the newsstand, he was the guy who generated a couple of bucks profit on a pack of cigarettes once every few days. To his nubile buddies at the orgy, he was another hole. Are any of those, however, really him? Do any of those do him any justice? No, because we are reducing him to a means to an end. We are using him to fulfill our own perceived needs. Like the city we try to get a view of in the previous chapter, we never really know him. All we see is just a projection of our own ego, what we think we need. It is a relationship with ourselves that does not honor him and does not ever take notice of his unique being.

This dynamic was so clearly evident in both of the relationships I discussed at length. Peter was on auto-pilot with me in large part because, as he put it, he realized a year or so into our relationship that he wasn't into white guys. I had spent uncountable hours, shared my home and my bed with him, opened my heart to him in a way that I had never done with anyone else, and it would not be a huge exaggeration to say that's essentially what I was to him after all of that—a white guy. Of course, basic physical traits are important for initial attractions that might lead to a romantic relationship, but how is that of any relevance once you already know someone? The point is that you don't really know the person you've spent so much of your time with for three years. What a lonely life.

This also raises the question about the myriad of other physical criteria by which so many people identify potential partners. I knew a guy who stuck to the only-blondes cliché. I never could understand what on earth that means. You see a hot brunette, and you're not interested? Think of how much of humanity he would cut himself off from with such an attitude: all of the brunettes, redheads, and raven-haired beauties in all of the world. Beyond this, imagine the eventual blonde my friend finds himself with. What is the underlying prejudice beyond his blondes-only policy that drove him toward her? Is he in love with her, or a blonde? Perhaps this is just my overly analytical side coming out, but I think there must be more going on here than simple physical attraction. I think the guy is having a relationship with his ego-projected view of what he expects a blonde to be like, and perhaps she is obliging by playing the part. He doesn't really know her or honor her being.

Was I much better? I was so busy projecting on Peter my need for a white knight that I either missed or ignored what he wanted. In hindsight, it was clear he was stifled in the relationship, uninterested in me, and looking for ways to escape. I was either so focused on my so-called needs and keeping my hands on him that I refused to let myself see or hear the truth. I told myself a happy story about his past in order to obscure the parts of his personality I didn't like and of which I disapproved. Although I am sure I knew more and cared more about him than he did me, the degree to which I truly connected with him was minimal. My love was deeply and sincerely felt, but it was for someone else, who existed only in my mind. I must be honest about this.

At the same time, what does this do to us, the ones projecting our egos? It enfeebles us and makes us lonely, because when we tell ourselves we need protection, support, someone to love us, and so on, we create or strengthen the self-fulfilling prophecy of our ego. We need protection or support because we are weak. Because we seek so-called strength in someone else, we reinforce our own perceived lack thereof. Of course, however, this is untrue. Unless we're talking about physical protection, which sometimes is a need for survival, what would happen to us without this sought-for protection or support, whatever those mean? This sort of self-talk serves only to convince us of our need and therefore our weakness, our failing. Of course we don't really need whatever it is we think we do; that's just a story we tell ourselves. Our basic needs are air, shelter, water, food. Someone supplying those to us does not constitute a relationship of love.

So what happens? Because we don't really need what we think we are getting from the other person, we're not satisfied. If we imagine we need someone to listen to us, and our partner doesn't do it, we become angry, sad, hopeless, or adopt some other negative state of being, and then we react in some way. We exact vengeance, complain to others, withhold love, and so on. Or, even if our partner listens to us intently, of course we are at best temporarily satisfied because that's not really what we need. So, we begrudge our partner for not listening more, or listening but not offering good advice, or listening to us and being too quick to offer advice. After all, we just wanted to vent, and the other person should have known that! No, he did know it, but always had a ready answer because he thinks he is so smart and is trying to trivialize our problems! It goes on and on and on. Our ego is getting stronger and stronger and obscuring our true peaceful humanity while our perceived need, and therefore our apparent failing as a person, grows.

This pattern is so prevalent that it hides in plain sight, taken for the normal state of affairs. To use a prevalent archetype, many women cite the following as the most indispensable qualities in their male partner: supportive, attentive to women, sensitive to their feelings, and so on. Although these are all undeniably positive and admirable attributes, the language used to express them is telling: "I *need* someone to listen to me and to support me." But, is it true? What would happen to this woman if her mate did not support or listen to her? Would she be a less efficient worker, a less loving mother, or less beautiful? Would she be less kind or generous? Would she love her parents and friends less? Nothing would happen.

In constantly telling herself this, however, she becomes convinced of its truth, and it is then a self-fulfilling prophecy. She selects the man who is the most supportive and the best listener, but because she doesn't really need those things in any sense, she will not be satisfied for long. Or, perhaps she picks the one who doesn't listen so she can keep the same bad-luck and-or victimhood story going. Remember the old trope that women tend to choose the guys that treat them badly? This is an expression of the ego's attempt to perpetuate itself. Then, she demands more patience, more listening, more support, and becomes angry or hurt when she doesn't get those things. In stressful situations, her need becomes activated, and she perpetrates her negativity on her husband, according to the dynamics of the cycle of pain. And that is the sickness of human need: we don't actually need what we think we do, and in fact these imagined needs are often bad for us. When we finally get what we only imagine we need, we want more of it or something else entirely after the inevitable disappointment.

In this cliché example, a woman with such faux needs would tend to be attracted to a man who would provide them, so what might this type of man be like? If he is not eventually turned off by the woman's neediness and ever-increasing demands for more support, he may have the complementary need, very common as well, to feel secure in his manhood. So, he validates himself by supporting the woman, telling her everything will be okay, pretending to listen to her, and occasionally setting her straight by acting as something akin to a father figure. However, as her dissatisfaction becomes more apparent, so does his failure to mollify her, and hence he feels like less of man. Something must be done because he tells himself that he needs a woman to make him feel like the big, strong, dependable man that society tells us men should be. Why then is anyone surprised when he finds validation of his manhood that he so "needs"—in the arms of another woman?

This is a simplified version of a story as old as anyone can remember, still playing out again and again each day. Far from supporting each other, these two characters wind up as complementary mutual parasites. They determinedly and compulsively attack each other's weaknesses in a suffocating choke embrace that people often mistake for love and devotion. It is, however, fear and desperation. The ego is doing all it can to survive, to maintain its illusion. Rather than strengthening one another, they weaken one another. What does strengthen, however, is their mutual dependence. They become crippled together.

Sometimes there is deep wisdom in old adages, however tired they may be. One of these is some variation of the assertion that one must love oneself in order to love someone else or have a good relationship with oneself before having a good relationship with someone else. Why is this so? In the example above, if the man loved himself, if he had an open, accepting relationship with himself, he wouldn't need the woman to validate his manliness. Even if he felt himself unmanly, improving upon that would be a task for himself alone. The woman might notice and compliment his improved "manliness," but he would not depend on her to prove the point. The woman, if she were comfortable with herself, would not need the man's support. She wouldn't need him to listen to her and validate her point of view or provide her constant comfort. Of course doing those things to one's partner is a kind act and common to strong, loving relationships, but the question here is one of need. If both of these characters could just love and accept themselves, they wouldn't need anyone's love to make their lives worthwhile, another person's validation to prove to themselves that they are enough.

Love is many things, but one of those things is the connection of two hearts, free of barriers, in an embrace of total acceptance. When that love is conditional on Harry supplying Sally's needs and Sally pretending Harry is something he is not in order to convince her that she is worthy, it isn't love. Therefore, true love, with nothing in its way, is associated with a deep sense of worthiness. When you understand that you don't need to be anything other than who you are, you stop, in the words of Brené Brown, "hustling" for love and acceptance. You stop pretending to be something you are not, and in that way you are totally honest with the other person, showing yourself fully for who you are. You never feel the inevitable resentment that would come with feeling someone else is forcing you to play pretend, deepening your sense of inadequacy. There are no such obstacles in your way when you accept that you are enough and do not require anything additional from someone else. That way, you can just love another person for who she is, not what she does for you. This is why you must love yourself first.

Love is also the most highly evolved, pristine form of connection, and connection is what gives meaning to peoples' lives. This then leads to the false assumption that we need to be given love by other people in order to feel whole. In fact, the reverse is true. When we feel whole, we are able to love other people, and that is how we connect. If we don't feel whole and therefore hustle for love, we don't actually feel loved, and we are too preoccupied with trying to earn love or trick people into giving it to us to actually love others or ourselves. And, because we are playing pretend, even when we are loved, it isn't really us! We cheat ourselves out of the joy of truly being loved: as was the case with myself. I felt increasingly unworthy of love. This is the law of reciprocity, another simple truth, We can get only what we can give, and we get only as good as we give.

The logic above may seem too neat and simple by far, suggesting some deception or at least that this is the simplified version: there must be something more to it. What my experience with the end taught me was there isn't. It's really that simple. In my state of despair and utter loneliness, what saved me was finally reaching out to other people rather than waiting for them to reach out to me. That was simple enough, but it extended beyond that. When those dear friends stuck by me as everyone else melted away, I was left with a deep sense of gratitude. I let them know how much their kindness meant to me, and I expressed my love for them. It was only that feeling within me and my expression of it that really made me feel loved.

I awoke to this truth as the grip of my depression slackened and my mood stabilized. At this point, I was able to spend longer stretches of time alone in conscious thought, contemplating my avid readings. I noticed that when I felt lonely and unloved, what made me feel better was calling one of my far-flung friends I had met during one of my many lives across so many countries. My history was full of these kinds of relationships, which I collected and treasured as some people do seashells from the distant shores they've visited. They are rarely at the forefront of the person's consciousness, but when the shells are from time to time removed from the display case, the memories and the feelings come to life as fresh as spring flowers. I called these friends and expressed to them how much they meant to me, and we talked of the good times we shared and the connection we had shared in that other lifetime far away. Suddenly it was I who felt loved. When I felt purposeless, I found something to do, however trivial, such as cleaning the dishes, and I put all of my attention into it. Upon finishing the task, my satisfaction at completing a job well done gave me a sense of purpose, however temporary. I felt useful by finding a use for myself at that moment.

In this way, if you feel unloved (disconnected), it is because you are not loving enough (are not connecting with other people). If you feel bored, it is because you are being boring. If you feel lonely, it is because you are isolating yourself and not reaching out. The law of reciprocity may seem harsh, but its simplicity is what makes it so hopeful. There are six billion people in the world, all beautiful souls trying their best, no matter how much their ego has twisted their personas. Go out and love one of them, and you will feel loved. Volunteer your time tutoring children or serving hot meals to the needy. Or, go love your dog, or even care for a plant. It sounds ridiculous, but try it. It really works. The world is an explosion of an endless combination of smells, tastes, textures, and sights. If you're bored, just go outside and look and listen. Turn your brain off and just take it in. You will not, you cannot be bored in that moment. If you feel your life lacks humor, start paying more attention to the goings-on around you. You will suddenly notice how ridiculous we human beings are, how absurd and full of irony everyday life is. When you stop being so distracted by your incessant inner commentary, the comedy and tragedy of life leaves you unsure of whether to laugh or cry. You will feel alive.

When I moved to Hong Kong, the depth of my depression had largely abated. My anti-anxiety and antidepressant medications ran out shortly after I returned from my project in the US in April of 2013. Though I was out of danger and my mood stabilized, much of the time I did walk around with a feeling of listlessness, numbness, and uncertainty. In these moments, I tested the law of reciprocity that I was reading about and was shocked with how rich the rewards from small gestures of connection could be. When I took my change and receipt from the cashier at the supermarket, I made eye contact with her, gave her a genuine smile, and said thank you. Instead of riding the back of the person on the queue in front of me, I gave him space and let him do what he needed to do with the groceries. I asked people how they were in a way that suggested the question was more than just a perfunctory greeting, and I listened to the answer. I held doors for people and let them pass, carried carts and bags for people up Central Hong Kong's treacherous cobble-stoned staircase-streets. This all opened up dimensions of humanity within me. I felt compassion for the older people struggling up the stairs, joy at making those peoples' days just that little bit easier by holding the door and reminding them that someone cared. This strange warming sense that we were all in this together pervaded my brief dealings with so many people. These brushes with humanity—when someone in the street moves into our space, often seen as an annoyance to be endured—became joyous little moments of connection for me.

Walking the streets, I turned off my headphones and listened to Hong Kong's frenetic symphony of urban cacophony. I looked at trees and signs and cracks in the road that I had passed by so many times over the years but never noticed or had seen but not acknowledged. I noticed the new buildings going up and the old buildings coming down in the city's never-ending reinvention, and I felt the change that is life. I felt so alive and so connected to it all. I know that this is difficult to accept and impossible to understand because it must be felt. So, I invite you—go try it.

These seconds-long windows into unadulterated life sustained me while I continued in my draining job, but after a year in Hong Kong, I finally left it behind for something much more people oriented and manageable. With my time in front of a computer reduced by at least two thirds, I integrated regular activities of focused attention and connection into my life: counseling students, volunteering, hiking in nature, exercising, writing. Living alone in a one-bedroom apartment, and traveling so frequently, without even a potted plant in my life, these seemingly trivial regular activities were all I required to satisfy my need for connection. Come what may, I can't imagine ever being lonely or bored again.

I now feel as if I have the basic tools to live, to navigate whatever obstacle course lies before me. To be loved, I must love. To feel connection, I must practice connection. In order to have the courage to love and connect, to show myself without equivocation, I must always feel worthy due to the knowledge that I am enough. When I know that I am enough and don't try to be something I am not, I see people for who they really are and not what I think I need them to be for me. Only then can I love them, and I can love them only if I love myself. It's a big circle. As with the virtuous cycle of embracing the unity of all things I described in the previous chapter, it all arose and the connections between the concepts all emerged and reinforced one another. Trying to simulate and recreate this process of enlightenment on paper ties my brain in knots. I am fully aware that the first part of this paragraph seems like bullshit that could have been lifted out of so many self-help or spiritual books. The reason for this, fortunately, is that it happens to be true bullshit. I do not think it is possible to convince you of this through any more logic or writing or even sharing of my experience, though I hope I have at least made sense. You need to just practice it. Try it. Do it for yourself. Satisfaction guaranteed.

Chapter 15: The limitless destructive potential of disconnection

If connection allows for love, what can disconnection inspire? In the rather limited relationship-from-need example already discussed in the previous chapter, disconnection in the context of a relationship can pervert what could be so uplifting into something destructive. Our man and woman, rather than strengthening, softening, and deepening each other through love instead weaken each other in a parasitic symbiosis, stifling rather than nourishing. Mutual support becomes dependence and eventually maybe desperate need, resentment, and disability.

This is a small theoretical example, but if we take it to its logical extreme, we could end up with a situation in which the two peoples' frustrations eventually explode in a dramatic fashion. We could have a murder-suicide. It sounds crazy, but just turn on the television: it's a rare but too common occurrence that happens every day. However, what will likely result is merely an ugly divorce or two lives consumed with an endless marriage of bickering and picking on one another—that is something much more common and relatable. In fact, it is so commonplace that it is taken for normalcy. Although an amusing cliché, isn't the archetype of the old married couple who never stops provoking one another more than a little bit morbid? Should people not be enjoying their life's twilight free of striving and worrying instead of constantly aggravating one another?

It is not an exaggeration to say that all evil is ultimately born out of disconnection. When we feel disconnected, we no longer feel the impact our actions have on others. The world and everything in it become means to the goal of manifesting our ego story into reality. And when we cannot connect, we cannot be empathetic or compassionate because we cannot feel with the other person. Eckhart Tolle (2005) expressed it succinctly:

> *If evil has any reality - and it has a relative, not an absolute, reality - this is also its definition: complete identification with form - physical forms, thought forms, emotional forms. This results in a total unawareness of my connectedness with the whole, my intrinsic oneness with every "other" as well as with the Source. This forgetfulness is original sin, suffering, delusion. When this delusion of utter separateness underlies and governs what I think, say, and do, what kind of world do I create? To find an answer to this, observe how humans relate to each other, read a history book, or watch the news on television tonight.*

At the extreme end of the spectrum, someone completely disconnected, completely identified with his or her own ego, is limited only by ambition, natural talent, and luck. Connection with other people and the love, compassion, and empathy it engenders no longer function. History and literature occasionally produce clear statements of such ultimate evil. Mao Zedong, murderer of unknown millions of people, with some rough estimates of 40 to 70 million, had ambitious plans for building a new Communist order in China. In a speech before the Party regarding his policy plans, Mao is said to have remarked,

> *In this kind of situation, I think if we do [all these things simultaneously] half of China's population unquestionably will die; and if it's not a half, it'll be a third or ten percent, a death toll of 50 million.*[2]

Mao was calmly talking about sacrificing tens of millions of people to achieve economic and political aims, and never in his lifetime thereafter was he found to have expressed any remorse for this. For him, people became a means to achieve his grandiose ends, and many millions more died for his schemes: including cultural reform, international geopolitical aims, and domestic political machinations. This was from a man who had no contact with average people and largely kept his own counsel.

An equally crisp statement of the worldview that can be supported by a belief in one's separation, a failure to understand connection, comes from C.S. Lewis' *The Magician's Nephew*, one of the Chronicles of Narnia series. Uncle Peter, a visionary inventor and magician, personifies evil borne by disconnection:

> *But of course you must understand that rules of [morality], however excellent they may be for little boys—and servants—and women—and even people in general, can't possibly be expected to apply to profound students and great thinkers and sages... Men like me, who possess hidden wisdom, are freed from common rules just as we are **cut off from common pleasures**. Ours, my boy, is a high and **lonely destiny**. (emphasis added)*

This is a fictional character, but his attitude is exemplary of history's great butchers—the Khans, Hitler, Stalin, Mao—who believed that they were different, separate, and above normal people. Humankind was a tool that was subservient to their grand visions, and normal morals nurtured by connection—empathy, justice, compassion—did not apply.

This is enormous evil, distinguished by its scope and macabre "achievements." Evil, however, is not defined by an act but is a state of being or the motivations behind it. For example, killing is usually an evil act, but killing in self-defense can be justified. The act itself is not evil. Similarly, suppose Hitler had never recovered from his failed Beer Hall Putsch and was instead laughed out of town like the village idiot, would he have been any less evil because he did not rise to the heights or sink to the lows he eventually would? Had Stalin died during some of the assassination attempts against him and not managed to rack up such an impressive death toll, would he have been less evil? If Mao had fallen off his horse during the Long March and never come to lead China, would he have been a qualitatively different sort of man? No. What made these men notable and notorious were their ambitions, their talent for achieving them, and a healthy dose of good luck along the way. What made them evil was their view of life, which stemmed from their conviction that they were separate. Their thinking merely represents a certain framing and indeed glorification of disconnection.

The view of evil as a form of disconnection also finds support in an entirely different discipline, the writings of M. Scott Peck, a psychiatrist writing from a medical perspective. He described evil as a "militant ignorance" of one's own "sins." It is not a commission of evil acts per se, but the refusal to acknowledge the pain they cause others. "Those who are evil refuse to bear the pain of guilt or to allow the Shadow into consciousness and 'meet' it. Instead, they will set about—often with great effort militantly trying to destroy the evidence of their sin or anyone who speaks of it or represents it." In other words, they refuse to bear the pain of their act, a pain that is felt only by empathizing and connecting with the one(s) they wronged. The only way to fully block that pain is to cut oneself off from humanity— to disconnect. They reject consciousness and tend to invent a story whereby their actions are justified. That story is their ego.

When evil is thought of in this way, it is clear there is a lot more "little" evil in the world that stems from the same sort of implicit or (more rarely) even overt reasoning. One who fundamentally does not recognize or rejects the connection of all things is limited only by one's ambitions, talents, and luck. The depth and duration of the disconnection fuels one's ability to perform wickedness. For an example of people with this sort of implicit reasoning, watch any interview of hardened criminals in prison. When asked about what they did and why they did it, what often becomes very clear is a sense of having been abandoned by the world, of total isolation. They are often remorseless because many of them grew up in terrible circumstances and had violence and pain perpetrated on them for their whole lives. Doing the same to others is natural for them because no one ever connected with their pain, so they are not limited by empathy. They of course do not verbalize it exactly in this way, but what we see are people completely disconnected from humanity—no love, empathy, or compassion.

For an example of someone who overtly sees the world as place of disconnection and indeed openly rejects even the concept of connection, let us turn to a familiar quote:

> *Josh, the difference between you and me is that you are a good person. You think about how what you do impacts other people. I don't. With all that I've been through, I've learned what a hard and terrible place this world is.*

So, I do whatever I want to get what I want...You have to be strong in this world to achieve things.

At some point, I understood why this statement by Gary stayed with me and so deeply disturbed me. Look at it next to Uncle Peter's quote above. This is the verbalization of evil. There is so much wrapped up in here that it is difficult to know where to start the dissection.

First of all, the statement represents Gary's worshipful dedication to his own ego. He is defined by his own sad story—that he takes "all [he's] been through" as a given and revels in it. He wrote a book about it. He lives by it. His ego does not have an unconscious grip on his mind, like the prison inmates above. He has been conditioned to be a hard and uncaring person who rejects the very idea of compassion, and he completely acknowledges and accepts this.

My being a "good person" is derived from the fact that I recognize my connection to and impact on other people—I think about how what I do impacts other people. Gary does as well, but he just rejects the very idea of allowing those connections to operate on him in any way. There is also a heavy underlay of isolation implicit in what he is saying. "All that [he'd] been through" has changed him, made him different than other people, strong. And, his behavior is all directed toward his desire to "achieve things." He advocates using people as means to ends. He of course justifies this with a sort of logic or philosophy, and in the end, when the people he hurts show too much pain, he cuts them off, not wanting to deal with the guilt or "meet the shadow." "I just move on," he said, and that's what he has been doing for years. This is "militant ignorance."

Recall for a moment Gary's cutting me off while he wanted to make up with his ex. Why? He did not want to feel the guilt that would arise from seeing the pain caused by what he had done to me. Knowing I was in a weakened, vulnerable state, he had made promises to me, turned my life upside down, and committed to me, only to abruptly call it quits without any visible emotion or care. He knew how devastated I was and did not want to see that or to contemplate why he had done it. Quite the opposite, he thoughtlessly dashed into another relationship immediately afterwards, going as deep as he had done with me, in an even shorter amount of time. He just refused to face his shadow. That's why he became so angry: because I didn't just behave myself and act like nothing happened. I fell apart, causing him to face his shadow.

On the other hand, recall that Gary wanted to make up with his ex. The difference between the two situations was simple—he did not feel any responsibility for the break with his ex. Indeed, Gary seems to have been the lesser of two evils in that case. Hence, making up or "forgiving" his ex required no feelings of guilt or responsibility. There was no shadow involved. Remember his reaction to prostitution in Thailand versus Singapore. The difference was he had used (and indeed gloried in using) a Thai prostitute. Therefore, he built a theory around prostitution being okay to justify his behavior and not face the shadow. He refused to contemplate some of what might have happened to that prostitute before working in a brothel. Feeling pity for the Singapore prostitutes was easy because there was not guilt involved. Again, there was no shadow. Those prostitutes in Singapore were those aforementioned hypothetical victims of Allied bombing whom Hitler pitied—even one of history's greatest monsters could feel guilt-free pity, a far more impersonal feeling than either guilt or empathy. Feeling sorry for them is cheap and easy if you bear no responsibility and do not relate to them.

If Gary's statement above is not evil, then what would be the meaning of evil? Though a statement of such moral clarity as to identify something as "evil" is a leap too far for most people, when I have recounted this quote to people I know, their reactions tacitly acknowledge the evil it expresses. When recounting some of things Gary said to me, people say things like: "Okay Hitler! Uh, sleeping with the devil, were you? All that was missing was the maniacal laugh at the end!" Luckily for myself and for the world, Gary and the countless injured souls who overtly and more often subconsciously subscribe to his logic are limited by their ambitions, talent, and luck. I of course caught the brunt of such heartless behavior to which this kind of a worldview gave rise in Gary, but luckily, even though I was in such a weakened state already, I escaped with only a few months of necessary therapy and some medications! Luckily for me I met an evil without much power, talent, or ambition. Seeing such dynamics so clearly in action was a fortunate experience for me—it taught me to recognize evil without facing big evil.

Weeks after I was first dumped, I was searching for an answer to why I was so disturbed by my relationship with Gary. Alone with my computer and unable to walk without pain due to my recent foot operation, I had plenty of time on my hands. I thought about the complete lack of empathy, on-off emotions, and Gary's other contradictory and strange behavior. I did a twenty- minute Google research project on the matter, and the word that popped up was "sociopath." I found the following often-cited traits and behaviors. [3] See how many apply to Gary:

- Lack of shame, remorse, or empathy. ("I don't [think about how what I do impacts other people].")

- General inability to react emotionally, ability to remain calm in what normally would be considered stressful or emotionally charged situations (for instance, complete coldness during his breakup, among many other strangely detached reactions he had to past events).

- Disregard for laws, social mores, or the rights of others. (If I hurt someone else, that's really their own fault because they allowed it to happen to themselves.)

- Unrestrained and impersonal sexual behavior, outbursts of self-indulgence (for instance, visiting brothels, episodes of casual sex).

- Frequent untruthfulness, misrepresentations, or insincerity (does not apply much to Gary).

- Unreliability (often late, missed appointments, did not believe in helping friends if it was an inconvenience).

- Poor judgment or failure to learn from experience (jumping into relationships immediately after breakups, going to live with a nearly complete stranger in Singapore).

- Superficially charming and sexy, especially at first (obvious given the attention Gary cultivated in the gay scene).

- Intelligent (good student, writer, banker).

- Manipulative, often gravitating toward soft targets; prefer to isolate people to gain control (previous boyfriend was much younger, Gary knew I was in a vulnerable state when we re-connected).

- Violent behavior (does not apply to Gary, though it's not hard to imagine he could exhibit this if it came out positive in a risk-reward calculation).

- Egocentric, incapable of love (rejected connection, did not consider others' feelings).

- Narcissistic (self-described as "vain," very focused on his appearance).

- Make frequent, uninterrupted eye contact. (He did.)

- Have few real friends. (Gary just "moved on" without caring what happened to people, he avoided getting "attached" to people, often criticized all of his "friends" when they were not around).

- Generally think rationally, free of delusions (never exhibited delusional behavior, and he described his actions and decisions in a very calculated manner).

- No clear life plan (never described any goals other than having a family and generally being admired and praised and did not express any clear concept of how to actually accomplish those things).

Other than the violent behavior and being frequent dishonesty, these traits actually apply very well to Gary. If not a sociopath, he was certainly more than halfway there. This is how twisted we can become when disconnected, and though Gary's situation is extreme, there are uncountable numbers of people who have failed to address traumatic circumstances in their lives, particularly during childhood. As they grow older, their pain and disconnection have a tendency to feed on their experience, further deepening their isolation and encouraging the festering of evil.

This is the little evil that pervades so much of this world—evil without spectacular results. Nevertheless, there is also so much room for hope and endless space for compassion, empathy, and forgiveness. There is no mystery about what went wrong. This is the cycle of pain in operation. Gary and the prison inmates have had such hard and sad lives, the accumulated pain of which has created the ego they have become, and they are simply passing it onto other people. This pain in Gary's case was caused by real, observable traumatic events, but that isn't relevant. Hitler was the consummate monster, and much scholarly work has been done to figure out where the product of such an apparently ordinary background "went wrong." Although a worthy scholarly pursuit and interesting for the analytical mind like mine, what difference does it make? It's just a matter of fact: whatever happened or didn't happen in the physical world, Hitler created a hell for himself in his own mind. Remember that pain is not real. We will never fully understand the accumulated pain he felt and what caused it, but that he felt it is undeniable, as he unleashed so much of it upon the world. As difficult as it would be for many, especially of that generation, to accept, clearly this was a man who was suffering immensely. As human beings, we must have a degree of compassion and empathy for him on some level, however much a monster he became. He didn't deserve whatever happened to twist his mind so, and the world certainly didn't deserve what he did to it. None of us deserve what happens to us, do we?

The question again arises: How to react to this kind of situation, when someone is perpetrating his pain on us? Again, the cycle of pain dynamics operate. On a personal level, a reaction that serves to displace our pain to someone else, whether it be offense, sadness, anger, impatience or some other form of negativity will serve only to further pollute the world. We would either pass our pain onto some third party or ratchet up the initial offender's negative emotions that caused the outburst. In my case, I hounded Gary with my sadness, disappointment, and neediness, hoping for…a second chance? Recognition? Guilt? In any event, I was looking for something for myself, not for him. The least I could have done was to respect his decision and let him go, to have been a pain sink and let it pass through me, thereby not adding to the sum total pain operating in the world. Though I do fear for other people who may fall victim to Gary's pain, there is little I can do to change that, and after all, he himself will be the one who will suffer the most in the end because only he has to live with all off that negativity. That is true in a theoretical sense, and we can infer from the specifics of his story what his future may look like.

The best response, however, would have been to react with love and compassion. Had I fully recognized at the time what a damaged person he was and been able to move past my own pain and ego obsession, I could have thanked him for being honest with me, given him a last hug. Unfortunately I was so emotionally frayed by so many dramatic ups and downs that I was in no position then to be so present. I have—however—changed. I have woken up. That can happen any day, any time.

This is the hope there is in evil. No one was ever born evil. People become that way as they spin the painful fabric of their lives into an imprisoning internal narrative. They invent a story that justifies their own actions in the cycle of pain. Nevertheless, at any time, there is the potential for the ego to dissolve, for them to wake up from their story. As pain sinks, we can do no harm. As beacons of love and compassion, however, everyone has the potential to enlighten the afflicted, who know not what they do, by exhibiting presence and love. A little brush with humanity can have the power to at least begin to break the hold that their accumulated pain has on their minds.

Thus, evil is not absolute—no one was born that way. *Pure evil* is an oxymoron. Every day is a new day, each moment is a moment: a chance for the evil to lose its grip and the person to awaken. It is a spectrum into which each person falls according to his or her ability to face the shadow and connect with the impact of his or her actions on the world. To do so is to acknowledge the connections of everything. According to Tolle, evil exists only in a relative sense and only in relation to good, as many other philosophies hold. It is the absence of good, just as cold is not a thing—it is just the absence of heat.

Therefore, we can flood and overwhelm this absence with our goodness. We can remove ourselves from or actively counteract the cycle of pain and therefore help to bring about this redemption. It all starts with compassion, empathy, and forgiveness for those who wrong us.

Recall, however, the process by which my healing took place. First I understood the concept—evil, disconnection. Then, I saw these clearly in Gary's example. Confronted with this, I was forced to look inward, saw it in myself, and I changed. When I looked back on my own behavior, I asked how many times had I allowed my fear and feelings of vulnerability manifest themselves as aggression, venting these without justification against a weaker or disadvantaged party? I had done this at work and socially. How many times had I dehumanized my perceived enemies (for instance, opponents in debates, people at the opposite end of political or philosophical spectra, members of "enemy" nations on the news) in order to justify injustice against them? How many times had I, in the words of Martin Luther King Jr, "sat idly by" and watched evil or injustice take place and said nothing, preferring instead to tune out the pain of the person being victimized? What I found when I examined myself was not pretty, but the perspective, the consciousness I gained has changed my behavior each and every day.

Evil is not inborn, but it is in all of us. We are all on the spectrum. How willing are you to face your shadow? The far end of the evil spectrum is observed when people become an empty vessel, devoid of goodness when disconnected from the endless potential for love and compassion that is humanity. At any time, that vessel can be filled. At any time, people can reconnect. We all can play a constructive role in that process by ending the cycle of pain and reaching out with empathy and forgiveness. As conscious beings, this is not our job—it is our nature and comes effortlessly once we too are connected.

Chapter 16: The limitless power of love

Love is the opposite of disconnection. Love between two people, perhaps the easiest love to recognize, is when two hearts become one. All barriers between them are knocked down, broken through, disintegrated. More broadly, love is the breakdown of all barriers obscuring the true self from anything else. Love is the painter painting, not for a grade in school, to earn recognition of some kind, make money, or support a political point of view. A painter in love is one who paints just for the joy of it, with no regard for what the painting will achieve for him. The painter instead brings his whole self to the work, free from any goals of the ego's construction. He becomes one with his work, giving it his full, pure, unadulterated attention in the moment. Even if at the end the painter is less than satisfied with the aesthetic result, the joy of doing it will drive him to return to the task. And, because his attention was completely focused on his actions, he will be able to know where and how he needs to change in order to produce a more satisfactory result next time. Contrast this with the painter who is working to become famous or make his fortune. He will stifle his creativity by making his work subservient to what he thinks other people want, grow embittered when he doesn't get what he wants, and come to see painting as a chore rather than a labor of love. Love is pure connection, and a life in pure love is one in which a person removes all armor and goes through it all without any falseness or disconnection. Accepting this kind of vulnerability would be pure courage.

This is why love is the most affirming experience a person can have. As fraught and flawed as my love for Peter became, there was a sincerity there that I do not doubt. I shared almost everything with him—my fears, my pretentions, my struggles, my hopes, and my dreams (that he rarely did so to me should have been a warning sign!). When I dropped my alpha-male persona before him and bared all that I could (I understand now how little I truly knew myself at the time), I found much I never realized was there. I had the capability to be generous. There was nothing I wouldn't have given to Peter. I had the capability to be selfless. I almost never thought about how a decision would affect me first, but rather him, then us. Though I got frustrated at his inability to articulate his feelings to me or at one of his outbursts stemming from his sense of inferiority compared to me, I usually felt compassion and understanding due to the gaps in his upbringing and education, only sometimes reacting to his aggression in kind. When I hurt him— even if I felt justified—seeing the pain on his face usually quickly brought out an effortless apology from me.

All of this shocked me. I had never thought myself to be a particularly caring or generous person. Compassion and empathy had never come easily to me, and indeed when I had previously noticed them in myself, I rarely expressed them, lest my weakness be revealed. And yet, here I was, willing to sacrifice anything for the person I loved. As I mentioned previously, I drew from the well of my soul and found it bottomless. I looked into the spaciousness of my heart and couldn't see the other side. This was unnerving for me, but it was also the ultimate affirmation. Despite my increasing desperation and hustling for his attention, in those moments when my courage allowed me to show myself fully, completely vulnerable and exposed, that is when I was most alive. That was when I was capable of doing things I never could before. I would not use the word *sacrifice* for these situations because, in line with the law of reciprocity, the more loving and generous my actions toward Peter were, the more loved and rewarded I felt. Even when he did not recognize or appreciate my efforts, rarely did I feel that I shouldn't have tried or that I lost something in the process, for I was giving things that have no limit. Love is the sun—showering us with its rays in no way diminishes it. The plants don't owe it anything in return, nor does it ask. I have not experienced this type of love since, and even if at the end of my life I never do again, it will have been enough for me. I shall bask in its warmth until the day I die.

This is the power of love. It makes us limitless. Does it suddenly make the clumsy person graceful, the blind person see, the sick person heal? No—we are limited by the physical realities of the world. But, because love means the breaking down of all barriers, it enables us to draw upon the strength and intelligence we didn't know was there. It's not that there's nothing we can't do but rather that there is nothing we won't try. The clumsy person will dance anyway despite his or her fears of looking foolish, the blind person will stumble as he or she walks down the street, and the sick person will find the bravery to try that new experimental treatment. When we love truly, in that moment we can say, "I love you" first, even though our ego fears rejection. This fear stems from the original illusion of separateness from the whole, which gives rise to the ego. The ego keeps us separate and therefore continually nourishes the fear. Love, however temporarily, allows us to put aside that fear and do what we didn't think we could. We start that business even though we know it may not succeed. We get on that stage even though the audience might not appreciate what we have to say. We put the words to paper because we believe that fiercely in the ideas, fully acknowledging that not everyone will.

Connection does all of this—it allows us to feel loving feelings, do loving things, and indeed *be love* when the barriers of disconnection come down. This is the natural state of things. We don't need to add anything. When our egos throw the walls up, that is disconnection, which in its most acute form leads to evil. There is nothing that love, the ultimate form of connection, won't do—look at Jesus, Mother Teresa, Martin Luther King Jr., and Gandhi. As illustrated in the previous chapter, however, the same is true for evil, the ultimate form of disconnection. There is nothing it won't do—look at Hitler, Stalin, Mao, Pol Pot, and Uncle Peter. What is the difference? In the former case, those paragons of love spoke about treating all, even enemies, with empathy, compassion, and understanding—in short, to connect. This drove each of them to act out of love and perform miracles in his or her own way. The latter group, on the other hand, emphasized what distinguished and separated them from others: their talents, their suffering, their vision. They fed their ego's notions of disconnection, empowering it to perform previously unimaginable destruction. It all boils down to the driver of the action, connection or disconnection. As the quintessential form of connection, love gives us the power to do the unthinkable, the unimaginable.

Typically, as much of literature expresses it, we are "struck" by love. It comes upon us unexpectedly. This indeed seems to be an accurate description for the most easily identifiable sort of love, romantic love between two people. Love too is also a practice. It is the practice of breaking down barriers, of consciously letting go or acting despite our fears. It is making the effort to give the other person the benefit of the doubt and trying to see from his or her point of view. When faced off in disagreement, think for a moment how the other person sees the situation. What are his or her motivations and fears? Putting yourself in the other's place breaks down some barriers and cultivates a little bit of understanding, therefore banishing a little bit of separateness. Maybe you'll find some of the tension and hard feelings between you dissolve just a bit. The next time you hesitate to do or partake in something you care about because you worry what people will think, do it anyway, and do it to the fullest. You may find yourself surprised by people's reactions, and if they react negatively as you feared, keep going because it's that important to you. The satisfaction you feel in the end will most likely overwhelm whatever negativity came out of the situation. These are simple practices you can consciously undertake every day to break down barriers and foster connection and therefore, love.

Love is a muscle you can exercise through conscious practice, and with it comes the power to do what you thought was impossible. Indeed, it is strength because you are confronting your ego-driven fears head-on, with the courage to be who you are and do what you want to do. As the barriers come down, you will be humbled by what you are willing to do. You will see courage and strength you never knew you had overcoming the fear that previously governed your life. Meanwhile, those who continue to live in fear erect barriers and become more disconnected. This disconnection, which is often taken for strength, is actually fear, which hardens into thick walls. This is the hardness of disconnection that cuts us off from feelings—the bad and the good. As this process accelerates, we are capable of greater evil. This is the logic of Gary as seen through the lives of history's great monsters. So, every moment of every day, the choice is yours: courageously practice connection and allow it to soften into love—or fearfully erect barriers that harden into disconnection and nourish your capacity for evil.

Part III. Epilogue

The path I tread

My life is different now. I start this retrospective recalling the words of caution in the introduction. Writing the first half of this book, the sad story, was painful. Not emotionally painful but tedious, dull, and mind-numbing. The person you read about was pathetic, wallowing in self-pity, and unable to see beyond the narrow scope of his own life, which became a cage of his very own making. The same repetitive thoughts spilled out onto page after page, unaware of themselves and in total possession of the thinker, who happened to be me at the time. Indeed, I must admit that had I read this two or three years ago, I would have put the book down in disgust, never even making it to the second part. "Oh please! Enough already! Who does he think he is? Doesn't he know that people have *real* problems? Buck up! Grow a pair! I'll reserve my pity for those who deserve it!" My reaction probably would have been something like that, but this of course was before I learned so much. I had thought then that it was my pity that I should give people. I didn't know what empathy was back then, or that its supply is endless. I thank you for making it through this far.

Each time I reread what I wrote, I am washed over by a wave of gratitude for what has changed. If I could put it as succinctly as possible, I would say I no longer have a "life," and no, I don't need to get one. Gone is the story, the narrative I put together to try and make sense of who I am, where I am going, and why I am alive. This is the same narrative that kept me stable and static for so long but, when overtaken by events, nearly killed me. It is the anchor to which I clung so desperately as the storm swirled around me and nearly drowned me. Instead of a life, I just have an experience, a simple consciousness.

What is missing from this consciousness is the endless chatter in my head, the ego, constantly judging, criticizing, begrudging, and wanting. Sure, it is still there, but my thought processes have abated by something like eighty percent. When the voice switches on, I usually laugh at it or, if I begin to listen to and reason with it, I snap out of it and come to my senses after half a minute. Just today, as I was in the gym doing repetitive exercise circuits, my mind wandered. "Look at that fat guy over there! What does he even think he's doing here?" it sneered. "Why doesn't he get off the machine so I can use it? It's not like it's doing him any good." Then, immediately thereafter: "Woah, that guy is outrageously built! What a loser. I guess he spends all of his time in here! Well, with a face like that I guess he needs to do something to make himself attractive to people." What woke me up from my nasty little reverie was the ridiculous cognitive dissonance in these unconscious commentaries on two people I did not know in the slightest. When I realized what had been going through my mind, I literally laughed out loud and continued my lifting. One. Two. Three. Four.

My ego did not let go without a fight. The turning point of course was the moment I walked out of that pharmacy and realized I was still alive. Nothing had fundamentally changed from the three minutes before when I had entered. But, from then on, as I read those books, saw the truth in the negative examples life had provided me, and then looked into myself, I was firmly on a path to consciousness. My ego was brought out into the light from the corners of my mind where it lurked, and it started to lose its hold over me. In those early days of my recovery in the first half of 2013, I would have wild mood swings. I would be sitting on the terrace of the building where I worked enjoying my lunch in the sunshine and then be suddenly seized by a rage over something someone did to me ten or fifteen or twenty years before. I would be enjoying a nice meal and be reminded that, much to my pleasure at the time, Peter used to put his culinary schooling to work in the kitchen, whipping up delicious meals. Oh, and so did

Gary. No one will ever do that for me again. There's no point in even trying. I'm going to need to… And then I would wake up.

I remember a thrilling long weekend jaunt I took to Tokyo in the summer of 2013. It was reminiscent of *Lost in Translation*, one of my favorite movies. The energy of the place was infectious, and the variety of activities I crammed in that weekend was incredible. I met a nice couple on the flight who took me to a great restaurant and showed me around the neighborhood near my hotel. I caught up with old school friends, seeing the new additions to their families and hearing about their exciting work and life experiences. As a single person, I was able to secure a last-minute booking at one of the city's (and therefore the world's) best sushi houses. It had only ten seats and normally had a weeks-long waiting list. Just one person, I lucked out because the other diners consisted of three couples and a party of three businessmen. The next day, at the Meiji Shrine, I was lucky enough to witness a traditional Japanese wedding, one of those ancient ceremonies that brings back the mystery and magic of a time that probably never really existed. I was captivated by the fascinating but just-large-enough-to-be-easily-digestible National Museum.

At the end of this exhilarating trip, I went out the last night and by chance met a bunch of models and wound up eating ramen at two in the morning, taking crazy pictures in those omnipresent *purikura* (Japanese photo booths) afterwards, and emerging half drunk and half asleep from a karaoke session with them as the sun rose over the vast urban jungle landscape. As I slept that morning, I woke up violently from a dream about the group I had just met. In the dream, one of the models started taunting me, and then the others joined him. In terrible shame, I was chased out of the karaoke session and wandered back to the hotel alone. Even when all was bliss, there was my ego again, working to devise a perverted interpretation of events that had just happened even as I slept, waking me up in misery after a wonderful three or four days. Like a cornered animal, my ego was most dangerous then, determined not to lose control. Luckily for me, these were death throes, a show of desperation rather than of force.

One of the practical methods I taught myself to unravel the stories was what I call story maps. When I caught myself thinking dark thoughts, almost always about the past, I would attempt to trace the story back to its origins, the initial sensory impulse which gave rise to it. What I found exemplified the elaborate acrobatics my desperate but cunning ego would perform in order to remain relevant. One day in the heat of Hong Kong's summer, I went to a shopping mall. It had an ice skating rink. It reminded me of another place I had seen the juxtaposition of heat and snow, New Zealand during the southern summer. My trip to New Zealand, you will recall, cost more because Gary canceled our Tanzania plans at the last minute. So, even though it was a remarkable trip, it was more expensive than it should have been, and the recent events tainted it with a definite sadness at times. I remembered a few of those free afternoons we had on the trip when the rain was pouring down and I was in my room crying, alone… And, there you go. Upon seeing an ice skating rink in a Hong Kong shopping mall, three seconds later I was back in my ego's mind hell, crying in a hotel room in New Zealand. The difference, however, was that with practice I would wake up and tune it out. The more I made these maps, the easier insanity's silent grip was to escape. Now, I find myself lost in thought only a few times a day and usually only for less than a minute.

As my ego has weakened, the self-fulfilling prophecies it spun have also unwound. One of the ego's tools in making its stories come true is to seek out and attract the types of people who will sustain the story. Thus, the person who formulates the always-the-sad-victim ego finds just the types of personalities who are happy to oblige that story by victimizing other people. In my own case, I had convinced myself that I needed to seek validation in the context of a stable romantic relationship, but the sad story was that I could never find the right guy who would appreciate and love me in the way I loved him. So, naturally I attracted and went after people who had terrible experiences in their past that had rendered them incapable of being in a stable romantic relationship.

Jonah had a series of tumultuous dramatic relationships that had made the gossip rounds over the years, supplementing his A-lister persona. Oliver had been repeatedly molested as a child by an employee of his father, a story that remains a complete secret to everyone who should know. Then, his parents had a traumatic divorce when his father's second family came to light, even though his mother still loves the father from afar. One can only hypothesize about the ways in which this type of childhood trauma might handicap someone emotionally and color his view of adult relationships. As a gay adolescent, Peter of course had been brought up by his peers to be a hedonistic gay cliché and had been taken advantage of by much older men, some of whom apparently were members of his church. His track record included not a single stable monogamous relationship. Gary had been betrayed, raped, semi-abducted and psychologically tortured. And there I was, wondering for years why the fates had damned me. Poor me, never able to find the right guy. The truth was that my ego was searching for these types of guys to perpetuate and strengthen itself, and these guys were looking for instruments to further their own stories. All of our parasitic egos happily obliged each other, so everyone's ego came away satisfied, while the host organisms were immiserated.

With the shift in my consciousness, the opening in my mind and heart, the entire vibration I give off has changed. I am no longer needful for anything from other people, so I don't seek out people to fill some perceived gap or shortcoming in my life. And hence, the people who have come into my life of late, though each has his or her own challenges, do not want anything from me other than for me to be me. Sure, I have met my share of so-called dangerous characters lately, but I find them to be so much more obvious, because in them I can recognize myself and the way I used to be. They want something from me, and although what it is can sometimes be obvious, it really doesn't matter. That they want something other than to enjoy my company is plain enough. As such, they do not pose any danger to my well-being. Someone can harm or take advantage of you only if either you are not expecting it or if you are actually in some way diminished by their aggression, grasping or other agenda. Because I no longer seek validation but rather simple enjoyment and sharing in other people, I have nothing to lose but my time in associating with them. I am more selective now because my mortality, and therefore scarcity of time left on this planet, became very real to me during my depression. I do not, however, fear other people's ill intentions or the negative side effects of their egoistic confusion. I know my ego is quite unlikely to take possession of me, driving me to respond in kind. One cannot dance the waltz without a partner.

One practical way I learned to get an early sense of people is actually by being less discerning. Trying to figure people out and guessing at their motives is both exhausting and inaccurate. Once again, you are not really getting to know a person but rather some vision of the person that you are constructing—using prejudices, past associations, accumulated experiences from other people, and so on. You are not honoring that person. Instead, these days I tend to take people at face value. Maya Angelou once said "Believe people when they tell you who they are. They know themselves better than you." This is right and wrong depending on who "they" and "themselves" are. Of course people all have a pure being, their true self, beneath whatever accumulated layers of ego they have, but the latter is what people think of as "themselves." So, if someone's ego builds a macho persona, you can bet he will be aggressive. This requires very little discernment, thinking, or judgment. Just listen to what he says and observe his behavior. Don't think of explanations or rationales—just observe. Had I been given this advice during the years I made excuses and equivocations for Peter's behavior and Gary's startling pronouncements of his philosophical views on life, things would have turned out very differently. See how others treat other people and remember that you are not special—you will eventually get the same if you hang around long enough.

Though I do indeed avoid people and situations that will take my time away from more joyful or productive alternatives, of course I cannot control who or what comes into my life. And, by ceding control of the largest portion of what happens to me, by surrendering, I am in much more control of what I actually can influence—my inner state. The stream of life ebbs and flows around me, and I go with the current rather than clinging to any anchors. However, I can steer and row in different ways to guide my direction but never fight the current—that will never work. In practical terms, this *sometimes* implies certain actions to "improve" my life, but it *always* implies a state of mind. To the extent possible, that state of mind is no-mind, simple openness, presence, consciousness—the state of awareness described any of these or other nearly synonymous words. As I spend so much less time and effort arguing with what is happening or what has happened, I am generally much better equipped to be present and deal with whatever life offers me.

Indeed, life has recently given me a number of particularly useful tests, insofar as they involved some of the same characters from the sad story. Their behavior didn't change. My inner state changed, and therefore my reaction was diametrically different. The best example would have to be the incident that spurred me to write this book in the first place. After years of no contact, Jonah came back into my life in 2012, when I was in Helsinki. He was traveling in the region during that time, visiting his then partner. Jonah connected with me again through Facebook. Given the years that had passed since our initial unfortunate courtship, I accepted his correspondence, and we did wind up catching up over email. When in the depths of my depression in Singapore, in between my surgeries and travel, he did meet me and take me out twice, something for which I will forever be grateful to him. However, I left Singapore shortly thereafter in early 2013, and that was that.

Late in 2013, after I was already settled in Hong Kong, he again contacted me. He had lost his job, was having difficulties with his family (people in Singapore tend to live with their parents until marriage, however late that might occur), and had another explosive, spectacularly dramatic end to his latest relationship (with the guy he had been visiting in Europe when we reconnected in 2012). I truly empathized with him and offered him my help. Given that his first language was Cantonese and he writes mostly about lifestyle topics, I figured Hong Kong would be a much greener pasture in terms of job hunting than Singapore. Further it would allow him to finally move out of his home and be a healthy but not-too-distant change of scenery for him. I offered him my contacts in the journalistic and literary world in Hong Kong and use of my apartment to save costs while he did his networking. I was still traveling all the time for work and had an extra bed anyway, so it was not much inconvenience for me at all.

Despite my request to do so, Jonah gave almost no prior warning of his arrival, and after arranging for a colleague of mine to pass him my key (I would be traveling that week) and staying up nearly all night cleaning my apartment for his arrival (recall that I typically worked until well past midnight), he informed me without explanation that he would be staying with another friend after all. I then made alternate plans to see him on Sunday, causing me to forego several other commitments. To make a long story short, he did not show up, did not apologize for his no-show, and later let it slip that he had spent his time in Hong Kong partying with his other friends and did little relevant to his job search. Internally, I felt some annoyance at having missed out on some other plans that Sunday, but mainly I just understood and felt sorry that he was clearly putting himself through another (easily recognizable) egoic cycle—wanting something, sabotaging himself from getting it, and then likely later citing the whole thing as another example of cruel fortune conspiring against him. So, when I very briefly met with him, it was perfectly cordial, and I wished him the best. There was no need to act—I genuinely had nothing but good will. He seemed to want a booty call. I did not pursue.

Wishing someone well and having positive interactions with him, however, is quite a different matter than inviting him into your life, especially across international boundaries. So, after that I cut off contact with him—there was no way for me to help him, and I had learned all that he had to teach me. After all that had happened—his initial treatment of me those years ago and now this latest example of extreme callousness—I figured my reasons for doing so should be clear enough. So, when he reached out to me again, promising another trip to Hong Kong "to see you," I called on my courage and decided to write him a brief letter explaining my thoughts. My intended two or three paragraphs became several pages, which grew into about ten. Though it started out as brief explanation for my decision to end our relationship, it slowly grew into a manifesto on my views on life and how they had changed. I cut it off eventually with a message of compassion and love but a sincere explanation of why he would no longer be a part of my experience on this earth. It was the first time I had put pen to paper and tried to map out and explain how and why I now lived my life and what my past experiences had taught me to get to this place. It was the seed from which this book grew.

The difference between my reaction, both inner and outer, at that time versus what I likely would have done prior to my awakening is so stark that it speaks for itself. Previously, I would have surely reacted to the situation with internal and external drama. I would have been hurt by his callousness and lack of regard for both my time and feelings. "Why did he do that to me?" I would have asked. When I met him, I would either have made an angry or a sad scene and demanded an apology.

This time, I was able to recognize my former self in his actions. This is classic egoic chasing of the tail. "I need to move on with my tragic life and get a job, so I will do everything possible to squander this opportunity to do both. That way, my sad story can continue, and I (the ego) will go on." Because I understood what he was going through and could keenly recall how that process felt within myself, I had compassion and empathy. I tried to do what I could do to help, but when it was clear that Jonah was not ready to receive my efforts, and other competing priorities for my time began to call, I said goodbye in a calm, peaceful, and loving way. In that situation, there was no further way I could be of service and nothing more for me to learn, so I extricated myself, with no residue of negative emotions, no sense of guilt that I had done something cruel, and no regrets for what I had or had not said. This particular attempt at egoic outreach, Jonah's ego's search for a self-validating reaction from someone, ended with me, and I did not add to the net pain of the world with a dramatic reaction. I never did find out exactly what it was he thought he wanted, and he probably did not consciously know either, but what difference does it make? He was somehow looking for himself, for some sort of ego validation in me, and I was not going to let him find it there. What a difference five years and a nervous breakdown makes, if you'll recall the drama from my first interaction with Jonah! Believe it or not, Oliver also showed up in Hong Kong at a similar time and did something equally inconsiderate and emotionally ambiguous, but I think one petty story is enough to make this particular point. I passed the test.

Even with all that I learned from my experience and the transformative process that followed, my ability to deliver this type of response did not come naturally. It was the culmination of this particular arc of change in my life, not the beginning. And, as my life will continue to be one of motion, there will be other cycles of growth and change hereafter. Compassion, gratitude, patience, and empathy are like muscles—they need to be exercised to grow and strengthen. The underlying practice, however, is one of presence. Rather than telling myself to be nice, it is more a matter of reminding myself to be here and not in my head. As the change was occurring, when enjoying the taste of a fresh fruit, I worked hard to stay there, not dream of the next meal, wonder how many calories were in it, or complain internally that I would prefer a different kind of fruit or in any way cheat myself of that unique experience. And thus I was grateful, appreciating the sweetness as it was. When someone such as Jonah slighted me, I avoided working through all of his potential ulterior motives or making the issue about me: what I did to deserve that, how I felt, how my time was wasted, and so on. All of these, anyway, are just thought products—rationalizations, notions of guilt or innocence, scenarios, and so forth. Instead, I concentrated on what I could do to improve the situation and recognized the pain driving the other person's separation, whether or not I understood his pain rationally. Hence, I felt compassion and empathy in my connection with him and his pain.

Standing on the queue at the checkout lane instead of growing impatient by thinking of all the things I could be doing with the extra thirty seconds I was wasting waiting for the slow cashier, I made a strong effort to turn my brain off and just take in the sights, smells, and sounds of the busy supermarket. I learned patience. This patience reinforced gratitude—how lucky I was to be there taking that all in— and allowed an opening for empathy as I felt the cashier's efforts in serving that long, ever-replenishing queue of customers.

The indispensable prerequisite that allowed this kind of growth, or more appropriately *deepening*, was the realization of my separation from the mind. Once I dispassionately observed the torrent of thoughts that were thinking me and recognized that I was not consciously generating them, I was able to not take them so seriously or allow them to govern my mood and actions. Occasionally I was startled at their aggressive nature or humored by their pettiness, but I was always comforted to realize that the voice was not me. I did not take them so seriously, and as the impact of the thoughts on my behavior and state of being waned, the stream of thoughts progressively slowed. The relative paucity of thought opened up a space in me that allowed virtues such as patience, empathy, compassion, and many others to flourish and support one another. This is the virtuous cycle I discussed earlier. One thing just supported another, and my readings as well as past experience reinforced it all.

This is the path I tread now. I regularly make wrong turns, stumble, and fall. I do find myself temporarily lost in painful thoughts about the past or fantasies about how I will make it right in the future. I will never really be lost, however, because now I know that I have already within me everything I need to find the way. I have access to a deeper intelligence beneath the voice in my mind and will always know that at any moment, when I am feeling disillusioned or disoriented, I can connect to the infinite depth of breadth of life all around me.

Where I am still stuck

Sometimes I still catch myself reminiscing about the past with some residue of negative feelings, but for the longest time I couldn't pinpoint what was stuck, the origin of the bad vibrations. I had forgiven, and not only did I believe that in my mind, but I felt it in my heart. I could look back and say with confidence that despite the immense pain I had felt, I was thankful for my experience in the end because it brought me into consciousness, into the beautiful present that I occupy. I did not blame myself for what I had allowed to happen, because I knew I did the best I could. I didn't know then what I later learned. Beyond that, I felt so powerful. I now understood the strength in vulnerability at the same time that my ego exerted so much less control over me. Without all of the preconceived notions of what I needed, what I deserved, and what life should be like, I dared to try new things, meet new people, and go new places because I felt I had nothing more to protect and defend. I had nothing to lose. For example, I quit my job and took a giant step off the career fast track in favor of something totally different that I enjoyed, felt was important, and paid half of what I used to earn. I completely climbed off of the career ladder. By emptying myself of so much of the heavy content of "my life"—all of the different facets of my ego—rather than smacking into the resistance I had previously put up, the tempest of life blew right through me. I felt so at ease. My armor deteriorated, and I found power in surrendering to life.

And yet there it was, the negativity. I dreaded bumping into the characters from my sad story, and from time to time either found myself lost in negative thought about the past or suddenly overtaken by some powerful negative emotion. When I did my story mapping, the emotion always led back to the same old sad stories. I was content to accept that this was just a stage in my growth and was grateful when I looked back and saw how much progress I had indeed already made, how joyful my experience was now. I chose to just let the issue lie.

I found insight, however, once again in my reading. This time it was a work of fiction that I had read way back in high school, *The Catcher in the Rye*, that awakened a truth for me. In that iconic coming-of-age story, Holden Caulfield is drawn to his misinterpretation of the lyrics of the song "Comin' Thro' the Rye." Though the meaning of the song is actually sexual, Holden forms an image in his mind of children playing in a field of rye, ignorant of a nearby cliff towards which they were all running. Holden says he would like to be the one who saves the children by "catching" them before they tumble off of the cliff (the actual lyric was "meet" not "catch," implying a romantic encounter in the field). This image provides the title and major motif that runs throughout the story, namely Holden's nurturing spirit and desire to save the children's innocence. He becomes angry when he sees curse words scrawled on school steps, because he doesn't think children should be exposed to those words so early in life. He cries at seeing his sister on the carousel because he knows he can't save her, just as he couldn't save his deceased younger brother, Allie. It is ultimately a fool's errand because of course everyone must lose their innocence if they are to survive, and living is inherently a risky business no matter how protectively parents, older siblings, or other guardians want to coddle us.

Harkening back to something I wrote earlier, I still feel sorry for myself, but not as *me*. I look back and feel sorry for that poor guy who was just doing his best, trying to do the right thing and make his way. And yet, he felt so alone, so unworthy. He suffered so much at the hands of himself and others who should have but also didn't know any better. I look at him and get angry because he didn't deserve it. What I realized is that as I was writing that letter to Jonah I felt very much the same thing. Here was a person I had known and observed over six years who always seemed to be in some sort of crisis or depression, constantly causing pain and drama for himself and others, always mixed up with the wrong guy in whom he sought comfort and validation. When he found me again, he was in a state of depression, and I felt keenly in my bones what that was like, and I wished there were something I could do to spare him from any further descent into the hell through which I had passed. I was observing yet another cycle of suffering for him.

And yet, suffering is the great teacher, the goad that finally drives us down the correct path at the fork in the road. I know this is true. There is, however, a part of me that refuses to wholly accept it. We all must lose our innocence, and we all must suffer in life. The process of conscious suffering is what teaches us and makes us grow softer, wiser, and stronger. Conscious suffering is usually preceded by long periods of unconscious suffering in which we harden, reject reality, and become more and more mired in the labyrinth of our story. This is the typical process.

However, I get stuck when I think about the depths to which I had to sink in order to finally get jolted awake. I get stuck when I see Jonah hurting himself in the same way over and over again over so many years, leaving the collateral damage of other human wreckage in his wake. I get stuck when I hear about Peter still trawling around gay saunas at nearly forty years of age and imagine him in twenty-five or thirty years still doing very much the same thing, his body bent with age, still seeking companionship, meaning, and validation in those empty rendezvous, his gentle heart locked away securely by the repeated act of sex without intimacy. I get stuck when I imagine Gary's future family, whatever man he has charmed into settling with him, nurturing his children with the calculated coldness, goal orientation, and grim logic with which he approaches life. Another poisoned generation fed from the cycle of pain.

I see all of this, and I wish there were something I could do to help them, to help us all. I wish that the process of suffering could be short-circuited, that the alternating arcs of painful shrinking and liberating growth could occur more gently, sparing the world of the dark depths of extreme suffering. I know this is not how it usually works. Read any of the spiritual books on my list plus the countless others around, and you will find nearly every author is the survivor of some tortured existential crisis in his or her life. Before the moment of insightful recognition, you will find irretrievable wasted years of lives, broken relationships, loss and violence, which cannot be made right. And, for every one of these stories that ends with the person finally walking on the enlightened path, you can find one (and probably in fact many more) unwritten stories without the happy ending—people who ended up in prison, suicides, or more likely, long lives of a slow-burn suffering. Then, at the end, when the turbulence of life has subsided, the racket of life's imagined drama quieted, a peace descends on the person. At that point, life becomes so simple. When there is nothing left to do, then one understands how small but how deep what really matters is.

This is why I sometimes become overly passionate or even angry when people come to me for advice. I often see the person repeating the same patterns of behavior over and over again, all the while the person is telling me she wants a different outcome. She keeps making the wrong decision again and again until the suffering is so great that she has no other choice but to change. Just like Einstein supposedly said, "Insanity is doing the same thing over and over again and expecting different results."[4] That is what the ego is—it is insanity, but it is taken for normalcy among people. I hate to see the suffering and just wish there were something I could do to break the insane egoic cycle.

The authors of whom I speak can usually look back on their suffering in a dispassionate way, even with a sense of humor. I can and often do as well, and I know that I am thankful for it in the end. I do wish, however, that it didn't have to become so painful, and I feel so sorry for that other person who was me. That is the past, however, and it is the present that concerns me. And, in these moments when I see suffering, I become like Holden Caulfield. I wish there were something I could do to save them all. I wish in some way I could just catch them before they go off the cliff, whether that be to the sad ending or to the dark depths that usually precede the happier outcome. Just like Holden's task, this is probably a quixotic quest, but in the process of writing it, I figured out that that is what this book is about.

Maybe I am not so crazy. After all, you can just go on Youtube and see any number of teachers, counselors, gurus, therapists, and other relatively enlightened souls, many of whom inspired me on my journey to writing this book, saying all the things I am saying and probably in a more eloquent way. Isn't that what they are doing— trying to teach people about all of this in the midst of their suffering or in a respite from a bout of suffering? Isn't the point to help people see, to prevent future pain and suffering, and hasten the harvest of a more enlightened life?

That, after all, is what brought me here, now. My friend passed me that book, and I was open to it. Maybe if I had seen it after my relationship with Peter ended, it would have made sense to me and I would have awakened earlier, before the trauma of my misadventure with Gary. Maybe then I never would have known the sickness of depression or come to the moment of suicide. But then again, if that were the case, I never would have been able to write this, and the one, two, five, or ten people who have learned something about depression and suicide through my survival would not have read it. So, maybe the depth of my suffering has made the world a little bit of a better place. I really don't know, but I do wish it hadn't needed to come to that point.

And, maybe Holden wasn't so crazy after all either. I know that since my awakening, since I dropped my skepticism of and opposition to life, I feel younger, lighter, and more innocent that I have in years. Gone is my suspicion, my endless second-guessing and analyzing of the reality unfolding right before me. Perhaps the single most startling and joyous change I have realized in myself is the wonder in small things I have regained from my childhood. I remember playing in the yard when I was five or six years old and being amazed and entertained by the way three twigs fit together so perfectly. When placed on just the right spot of a rock, they made a little sailboat. I rode in that sailboat all the way into the sunset on the endless horizon. The loss of this kind of imagination, replaced by a limited sense of reality, is one of the starkest and saddest aspects of the transition from childhood into adulthood. Now however, the frequent silence of my mind allows me to walk through a park or down a sandy beach and notice all of the colors and shapes, the dancing of light and shadow, the infinite number of textures, the smells and the sounds. I can just walk and take it all in and be inspired almost every day, if not more often. On these occasions, I can't help but thank God that I am alive and not dead by my own hand, and I know that I love and am loved. That is something like innocence, isn't it?

So, here I add my voice, such as it is, to the growing chorus of the New Age. Nothing I have to say is any different from what has been said before. I am not so ignorant as to think there is any new philosophy, revolutionary logic, or deep magic in any of my thoughts, words, or deeds. All I have to offer is my unique experience. Carve the holes in a flute ever so slightly differently from other flutes, and you will create a new music different from that of every other flute ever made. Life has shaped me in such a way that this is how the voice coming through me sounds. The source of the voice is universal and never-changing, but it just sounds a little different coming through me. I hope this unique voice can reach someone, so that he or she never reaches the edge over which I almost plummeted.

A Plea

Often books, songs, works of art, or any creation have a very different impact from what the person inspired to create them intended. Upton Sinclair wrote about the meatpacking industry in Chicago intending to spread socialism in America. Instead, America got food safety regulations. That is part of the fun of life: we never get exactly what we expect. And, when we make our mark, it is like the woodpecker, who pounds a hole into the oak. Two hundred years later the oak still bears the mark, but the bird is long gone and forgotten.

Maybe nothing I have written will make any sense to anyone who actually reads this. However, if I can hope for anything to come from this book, it is just that anyone who reads it gets better informed about depression. Depression is the unfathomable black hole that devours all the light of the universe. It cannot be understood but by the person who experiences it because it is an insanity unique to each person it afflicts. It is just the ultimate triumph of the insanity of the ego that, in its less-extreme manifestations, is so common as to be taken for normal. It truly is a mental illness about which there is so little awareness and, consequently, little empathy. I myself had been a chief offender in this regard prior to my breakdown. I always thought life was too short for wallowing. I always wondered why people let the small stuff get them so down, while so many others have had worse things happen to them and have come out fine in the end. This is the external view, but depression, like all insanity, is a purely internal and ultimately not real. We cannot see it from outside because it's a sickness of the mind.

So please, if you know someone who is down and cannot seem to get up, be there for that person. Listen. Ask questions. Do not argue or try to convince. Just be there whenever you can. Touch the person if he or she will allow it, because physical contact will remind the person that, however lost in the mind the person is, he or she is not truly alone. The warmth of the human heart perceived through a gentle hand may be enough to wake the person, however temporarily, from his or her nightmare. And, when you're doing this, please do try and get the person some professional help. Many health care plans cover mental health, and if his does not, there are so many resources available. There are charities, hotlines, religious organizations, guidance counselors, school psychologists, and clergy.

Please, whatever you do, do not leave the person alone. In those terrible days after Gary left me, I was alone with my physical and emotional injuries, cut off from human contact. My friends disappeared or even betrayed me when I needed them the most. My real friends, who would have cared for me, were all unfortunately far away. In my isolation, my mind took over and spun its stories right down into hell.

I know I was a nightmare to deal with in those days. I talked endlessly about the same things over and over again (as Section I of this book exemplifies), but I was only verbalizing the endless though loops playing in my mind. Remember, depression is by definition completely self-involved. For the afflicted, everything that happens is a negative reflection of the sickness inside. This is why I am so grateful to those people who, when they came back from wherever they were, had the patience to take me in, to listen, and to pass the unbearable hours with me until I was in the good hands of professionals.

I am alive, but so many aren't. Suicide claims the lives of over 100 people per day in the US alone. By just spending even half an hour getting educated on the subject, paying enough attention to spot the signs of depression and being there for the sufferer, you can save a life. By saving a life, you can save the world.

End Notes

[1] In that episode, Gary again met a much older man on the internet when he was looking to move from Taiwan to Singapore. A complete stranger other than internet contact, Gary relocated to Singapore, moving into his house rent free and accepting the man's assistance in finding a job. The man of course wanted something in return and was clearly interested in Gary sexually, but Gary rebuffed his advances while accepting the man's job offer at a reputable company. Over time the man was able to access Gary's phone and computer contacts and chat histories and used the information to constantly call and follow Gary, assuming fake identities. Gary became traumatized and afraid to leave the house that belonged to his anonymous tormentor. Of course Gary had initially attempted to manipulate the man, but the outcome was just the reverse. This traumatic episode lasted around a year and resulted in a number of Gary's noticeable personality traits, such as his extreme reaction to being startled.

[2] There is some dispute among historians over the context and exact meaning of Mao's words.

[3] There is however some confusion in distinguishing that term from *psychopath* and does not appear to be any official list of characteristics or diagnosis defining a sociopath from the numerous professional psychological organizations.

[4] The actual origin of this quote is unknown.

Made in the USA
Middletown, DE
17 June 2021